Thirteen Tangos For Stravinsky

Previous Titles by the Author

romance de agapito cascante   repertorio americano, costa rica, 1954

the gathering wave   alan swallow, denver, 1961

the flesh of utopia   alan swallow, denver, 1965

menashtash   little square review press, santa barbara, 1969

agapito   charles scribners, new york, 1969

words on paper   red hill press, los angeles, 1974

spain, let this cup pass from me   red hill press, los angeles, 1972
(translation of césar vallejo)

two elegies   red hill press, los angeles, 1977

the half-eaten angel   nodin press, minneapolis, 1981

when i was a father   new rivers press, saint paul, 1982

miss o'keeffe   university of new mexico press, 1992
(collaboration with
christine taylor patten)

four poems about sparrows   eyelight press, cordoba, nm, 1994

a garden of sound   pemmican press, washington, 1996

a history of light   sherman asher publishing, santa fe, 1997

Thirteen
Tangos
for
Stravinsky

alvaro
cardona-hine

SHERMAN ASHER Publishing

Acknowledgements

"The Attic," "The Persimmon Door," and "Betty Croft" have appeared in *American Writing* issues 6, 9, & 10. "Dr. Alfaro" has appeared in *Chelsea 51* and "Portrait at Teatime" in *Gulf Coast*.

Cover Design: Janice St. Marie
Interior Design: Judith Rafaela

First Edition
ISBN 1-890932-07-8 Softcover
ISBN 1-890932-11-6 Hardcover

Library of Congress Cataloging-in-Publication Data
Cardona-Hine, Alvaro.
Thirteen tangos for Stravinsky / Alvaro Cardona-Hine.
p.   cm.
ISBN 1-890932-07-8 (alk. paper)
1.Cardona-Hine, Alvaro—Childhood and youth.
2.Costa Ricans—California—Los Angeles—Biography.
3.Los Angeles (Calif.)—Social life and customs.
4.Poets, American—20th century—Biography. I.Title.
PS3505.A655Z474   1999
818'.5409   99-14220
[B]—DC21   CIP

Sherman Asher Publishing, PO Box 2853, Santa Fe, NM 87504
Changing the World One Book at a Time™

for my sister Ana

...I came early
   when it rains the persimmons are
   astonished....

                    from *Mobile for Los Angeles*

CONTENTS

FOREWORD

Alvaro Cardona-Hine is a natural-born wonder. I would use the word genius, but he demurs—demurs, I suspect, because genius is too egotistical a word, too narrowly mistakes the fountains of beauty.

Or of life. As if there were a difference.

Alvaro is, nevertheless, several sorts of genius. Just so you know. In his music, in his painting, and in his words, there is that indwelling, that clarity and celebration, that ghost of the north wall's winter shadow blue on the snow, that summer simplicity of daisies in sun, that laughter of saints and masters, those yellows of persimmons and apricots, that plain humanity with its dirty fingernails and inconsolable longings, which we must call genius.

He is the sort of genius who makes you want to write paragraphs like that.

He is a genius, among other things, of lost time. "Time is so disordered," he said the other day. "How strange it is to be here, in this time of my life." I think he meant that there were other times in his life, as in all our lives, and how curious and nonsensical a thing to have this "I," this incredulous and all too credulous and never credulous enough witness (to have it penned up merely in these latter moments—this one only moment) how curious that it should be now, with these beautiful vistas of a life seen from a certain altitude.

In *Thirteen Tangos for Stravinsky*, he says, early on, "I sense the pulse of things that have fully been and are no more, so that I know the same goes for me, that I am young by chance as it were."

As we are old by chance.

Thirteen Tangos comprises a suite of brief memoirs covering the period of his life after his family left his beloved

Costa Rica hoping for a better life in the States until roughly his high school graduation.

"I am stuck," Alvaro says, " . . . in the static ways of the visionary. My nature is to see one thing and have it reverberate outward in concentric light rays." His stuckness is our luckness. In metaphors of incredible flow and elaboration, we glimpse shimmering facets of entire diamond worlds. These are metaphors you wish to linger in for a while, struck by the dazzle, the beautiful flashing of an unparalleled love for life. That love for life has, for once, met its proper host in the sweet singing of words.

In other words, you don't rush through this book. The way you don't want to rush through your life, noticing nothing, miserable and driven. The way you do want to rush through this preface, which is, believe me, just a warm-up, just a gentle loosening of the mind and spirit so you won't pull something when you dive headfirst into the ungravitied freedom of Alvaro.

There is a story, if you want one.

We follow the hopeful young man entering the United States past "the gangly officials waiting by the gangplank who will shortly take us to their bungalow . . .doubting the identity of the insignificant looking man from the banana republic and his insignificant looking family . . . unhappy at having to let us in."

Dolor and hope: "We will have to enter," he says, "on tiptoe, past ambiguous arms." But they enter with such celebration, such willingness. Far from castigating his adopted land—though he sees more clearly than most its flaws and shallows and empty realms of the spirit—Alvaro sings it to life.

The boy we see growing into a young man is full of dolor and hope, of passion and wonder and muteness. He studies biology for Miss Kennedy, one of his heroes, lost in the heroism of Pasteur and the sexuality of microbes. He slowly learns English. What a pleasure it is to perceive so beautifully, from the vantage of his fifty years of increasing poetic mastery, that early speechlessness, so discouraging to the young Alvaro, to us so clearly such a marvelous door. And speaking of doors, one may begin to understand here, reading "The Persimmon Door" the second chapter in the book, a little more of the charge and sensuality and wide blue time of Alvaro's golden paintings of persimmons—how it is that he has changed time and possibility into color.

This young boy falls in love, repeatedly—with the young woman who teaches him English—and here I cannot help but think how the singing heart of that Spanish-speaking boy awkward in English, how that singing heart accepted my own language too and made from it and through it more lovely songs of praise and gratitude than I have dreamed—

Lost my sentence there. The boy falls in love with a tantalizing and raunchy waitress who dates sailors but teases, with naked perfume, the wise innocent, who is saving himself for a proper readiness. He falls in love with a girl at the school bus-stop. He can speak his love no more than he can speak his art. He doesn't know what he is, or what he may become. Wonderful and terrible people appear and disappear. Dr. Alfaro, whose blubbery substance is all show and no substance, but who becomes all of us in his total lack of humility, his humble acceptance of the shape of his own preposterous and sham-filled existence. The intensely devoted couple, the whole world a music of love before them, who rent from Alvaro's family briefly, until the woman is struck down crossing a boulevard, as emptily, as meaninglessly as the Great Dane struck by a bus years later. Mr. Footernak, who, with Alvaro's dear mother, showed the seventeen-year-old young man what a sparkling wildness of appreciation might glint and whisper under decorum: "My impatience with formal learning, a kind of unfortunate disability or perhaps simply the inability to see how harmonic rules relate to dream sound, has led to my . . . clinging to these two people in the afternoon . . ."

And oh yes the Japanese attack Pearl Harbor and there is a war and the family moves to Mexico City fearing assault on Los Angeles but are lost there and the young boy becomes hooked on horror comics, and the world rolls on and they return to L. A. and there is high school and there will be college and the great American fifties, and you get a good look at how empty our schools are and how thoughtless our immigration policies are and yet how all-accepting our mountains and cities have been and are—

But—

But this book is about the real things.

To say that *Thirteen Tangos for Stravinsky* is about loss and longing is to be deeply misleading. It is, but it is more nearly about what need not be lost. "Death is the mother of beauty," Dylan Thomas insisted. I don't know that I have read a more touching love story than the young Alvaro's adoration of the shoulders of Jo Wood on the school-bus, an adoration which finds its total and complete fulfillment when she signs his yearbook on the last day of school, the last day he will ever see her.

This is a book full of mystery, charm, and—again— hope. The best hope, the only hope there is. It is rich with the inwardness of every single moment of existence, be those moments properly observed. The richness is like the richness of a kaleidoscope shaken so that its only imaginary jewels tumble forth in a cornucopia of radiant seed. It is rich in its lists and metaphors. I would love to quote you passages at length, but the problem would be where to stop. I would wind up quoting you the entire book. In fact, that is precisely what I think I will do, just as soon as I finish the preface: I will quote the book to you, from the beginning to the end, entire. Be sure and take a look.

But for now I may say, watch for the incredible lists and metaphors, how they spill gloriously, endlessly out of the mouth of time, how they keep turning corners into new world and doors and ways of being.

There yes is a story in this book, but not a story that one should hasten through. I urge the reader to read the book quickly once through, if a quickness of understanding, a generality of impression, is somehow necessary. And then to spend the rest of a life wandering its hallways, and arrant and miserable alleys, and intoxicated backstreets and gardens, one slow afternoon at a time.

It is appropriate that this book takes its name from another adoration, this one the young Alvaro's undiscriminating adoration of music, his overwhelming need to compose. There is a short and fortuitous and anxious meeting backstage with Stravinsky after a Hollywood Bowl concert, and the young boy dreams of writing thirteen tangos for his idol, and taking them to Stravinsky's home, and having the master play them on his piano . . .

Those tangos were never written, were only conceived.

But for Alvaro, what is conceived is real.

This book has thirteen chapters, thirteen beautiful chapters full of dreamy passion and multifarious bewildering precision. Stravinksy, if he had heard them, would have been blown away, as if by his own music as it came to him and chariot-lifted him into the crazy persimmon mirrors of heaven. We cannot be certain that Stravinsky is able to hear, so you and I must listen for him.

We must listen closely, and lose ourselves.

Jack Butler,
Co-Director of Creative Writing Program
College of Santa Fe
Santa Fe, NM

1
THE ATTIC

The year is two-thirds done but, for one such as me, twelve and still a boy, it hasn't even started; it is the youngest, freshest 1939 ever: it is like a gill-less mushroom, like the odor of dawn before it has popped out of the gunnysack, like the faint iridescence in the genes of the magpie (promising that glint of blue on its wings).

For those old enough to know suffering, Asians, Europeans, the decade is almost over and a new and more terrifying one is in the offing but, for me, because the world is inordinate, a constant flowering is taking place. Every cell in my body is calibrating an eventual man. I am going to be hurled against the light of a thousand windows.

Off the California coast, autumn is a green-grey wavering of dolphin water. All day long, we toss, heave, go up and down; gently we plunge and rise into the luminous haze of the marine sun. Praise be this wrenching.

The Norwegian sailors give me green apples to munch on. They smile their wonderful foreign smiles at my younger sister. We've been at sea ten days and the immensity has taught us that one can play at the edge of the abyss. Spray turns into sudden seagulls, everything astern of the boat bubbles up white, crocheting the dress for distance as it weds the past. The decks are slippery, the railings barnacled with untold coats of paint, but the Pericles, this somewhat middle-aged freighter, seems to want to plow the seas forever.

Today we have been promised land by a captain who doesn't lay great store by arrivals. He is a little contemptuous of any-one who believes that journeys come to an end. He is even contemptuous of the Pacific, preferring the thunderous Atlantic to our idyllic buoyancy. For the next few years he'll probably consider the inky Germans lurking in its depths just another challenge.

But we have been served fish every day for lunch and dinner and have had it with herring and dry cod cooked alongside uninspired potatoes; we are tired of sardines and roe and the multiple other saltinesses of the sea. My mother's dream is on the verge of threading its own needle: California as the prom-ised land of fruit and plenty, versed in golden meadows, awash in Whitman's vision and tongue.

This vision had been held up to the children on my mother's side of the family, the Hine Pintos, as the *ne plus ultra* of exist-ence. They, the older generation, had been brought up Califor-nians until being forced to return to Costa Rica when a relative swindled them out of the family coffee plantations. My grand-mother and her sisters, soon orphaned and destitute, survived by starting their own school where they taught English. From infancy then, Mother and her brother and sisters heard San Francisco and its ruralities at the turn of the century extolled in that passionate fashion that childhood and regret lend to things praised.

California became for my mother, the most industrious and adventuresome of the siblings, something between a dream and a goal. She saved money half her life in order to raise her own children in an environment conceived as magically open-ended.

When it was finally possible, my father, who had worked in the Costa Rican congress taking down meaningless speeches for some twenty years, went and asked the president of the republic for a post as consul *ad honorem*. Since this was a token recognition, with no pay and actual duties, he was granted the consulate in San Diego, a place where it wasn't needed. Los Angeles, where we wanted to settle, already had a real consul.

With a diplomatic passport, which enabled him to settle anywhere in the country, he could do as he pleased. Nobody need know that his wife (putting the English she learned under her mother's tutelage to good use) would go to work in the garment industry for starters.

This brief background, which doesn't touch on the greatness of Francisca Pinto de Hine, will have to explain what we are doing floating off San Pedro. I am leaving my grandmother out of the picture because she is not floating along with us on the Pericles but, instead, has remained back in Costa Rica, on the porch of her house in the Barrio de Amor, waving a handkerchief as we pull away in a taxi. I leave her there until I can take up her cause and her beauty again, and at the proper time sing her praises as they should be.

Mother, Father, the captain and an American couple are in the dining room playing poker. The afternoon is listing badly when my sister and I spot a vague outline of low and insignificant hills. Could they be our destination? The glorious United States of America? Nothing could look more disappointing, more barren, more unsolicited. With a sort of unmanageable childish dread we rush to the dining room to report our sighting. The grownups barely take their eyes off their cards although, upon our insistence, Father, who has only a pair of deuces, puts his cards down and walks out with us to check the thing. He is probably equally disappointed in the distant hills but all he says is that he and Mother will join us in a little while.

For the next forty-five minutes my sister and I are witness to how slowly a mighty ship like the Pericles is able to draw the continent to itself, pulling and shoving, like some proverbial beetle, its ball of dung. The dun-colored hills don't cooperate in the least, anonymous and sullen like a paralyzed horizon of crocodiles. It is the ship instead which has to come to Mohammed.

The port is also pretty much the sleep of mediocrity. An increase of seagulls circling above abandoned forklifts and cranes, the fist of the sea uppercutting a mean thrust of senseless rock, a sun warming up the grey soup of the day on the backburner stove of those hills which promise nothing but to be inherited, claimed.

In my heart, besides the matriarchal maze of love now lost forever, the specificity that was my life sucking the nectar of trumpet vines, filling my mouth with loquats, hearing the breeze rattling its sabers in the canefields, diving into an oxcartful of coffee berries, catching the smell of sweaty horses, eating duck eggs, all of that and ten times more gets reviewed in the name of regret. Looking at those empty hills we are facing as if they were a firing squad, my minuscule life passes before me. I see the schoolyard which I and all my school-mates emptied the minute we graduated, not knowing what happiness was, what the smell of newly sharpened pencils meant of a kind of olfactory ecstasy preceding the written word with more poetry than all its subsequent so-called meaning, and I feel the first twinge of a tachycardia that will emerge fifty years later as the end result of my exile.

With sweaty hands holding on to the ship's railing I look at what I am entering and at what I am forfeiting, fifteen hundred miles behind. At this moment, lacking all perspective, I would turn and run back. Fearful of some monstrous emptiness, some coming, disgraceful crassness lying in store for me, I feel weak and disillusioned.

I do not know how quickly relief is on the way, how quickly my eyes will open wide on the margins of a new life. It is all there, just on the other side of those blank hills, past the gangly officials waiting by the gangplank who will shortly take us to their bungalow and paw through Father's papers, doubting the identity of the insignificant looking man from the banana republic and his insignificant looking family, glancing at each other and shaking their heads, unhappy at having to let us in.

We will have to enter on tiptoe, past ambiguous arms.

I stand at the railing beside my parents and my sister Ana and I look. I want to go back to what I know now was the stupendous richness of my days and I know it is impossible. So I look, I keep looking. I want a clue, a hint of milk-kindness, but the entire future is veiled, inherent in nothing physical. The world is just at that moment more mysterious than ever. Through a tiny fissure in its imponderability, if I could only see, I would witness the delta of my life opening there, waiting: gardens, children, harmonies, blessings, mistakes, friends, lovers, barbers, canvasses, idolatries, knowledge, forests, wisdom, petals, spiders, drunks, rivers, automobiles, bullies, mountains, laughter, jobs, neighbors, silence, incumbrances, all interrelating, preparing, organizing themselves for me and through me and with me, leading their independent existences in streets and houses and wombs, in dusty country lanes slowly turning into urban sprawl, in groceries still absent from the market, in classrooms warm with boredom, in radios beginning to play sugar to my ears.

At this moment, shadows demanding flesh, voices sealed in silence, encounters, gestures and disasters, the infinite lotteries of chance are summed up, frozen, beyond those hills, waiting, forming, gathering force. I grip the ship's railing and paradoxically catapult myself beyond the hills. I see Celia Zeledon, neurotically running her boarding house with worry-spittle and star. And her husband, round of face, benign, going to market and getting me candy in accordance with instructions she gave him in English and which I proudly deciphered, understanding, for the first time, a little of the world: How she wanted me happy so we'd stay with her longer.

There is that first ride, through thirty miles of Nuestra Señora de los Angeles, past the parallel miles of palm trees, the bougainvilleas drowning the bungalows, the poisonous oleanders flowering white or red, and I begin to understand. Everything is lurking with codified embarrassment. A grey cargo ship puts in at harbor and four lower middle class immigrants disembark, ogling everything and wanting, like lay tropical Popes, to bend down and kiss the ground. For two hundred years it has been happening to others but now it's for real because I am the protagonist. San Pedro is an inner tube lying half submerged in rain water. The immigration officials, alert as Brillo pads, are scratching their heads, puzzled at the woman with the tight mouth, the old boy with the consumptive look, the fretting eaglets. Do you let them in?

The cranes are playing Narcissus on the syrupy water, going deep into the ship's hold and bringing up all sorts of burlap things and I am trying to focus on this past-future business through a moment which blurs and comes into focus unpredictably.

Celia's boardinghouse is a tired, three story high mansion (mansion by our standards), whose porches and turrets have that certain Japanese look typical of California bungalow houses. It speaks for the leisure of an America identifying itself with silent movie ethics and Prohibition. Exploring it is going to take Ana and me some time.

Meantime, in the following days, we venture out. It's a stunning world of manicured gardens and lawns curving down to reach the sidewalks, of bushes jammed with orange-red berries and robins and blackbirds everywhere. The air is crisp. We look forward to winter, to sweaters and coats, perhaps even gloves. So much that is exotic! All we bring with us is the warm embrace of constancy all year round, the even weather of tropical mountains. Here, one glance at the San Gabriel Mountains tells us how close we are to that magical, celebrated stuff we've never experienced called snow. And we marvel at the sprinklers in every lawn, how they bathe the robins, how they spray water brought from even more distant mountains.

I am so overwhelmed by the beauty of this clean, quiet, orderly neighborhood that I don't see the lack of neighborliness. On the contrary, the lack of fences or high walls between properties appears Utopian. It is totally unlike the Spanish sense of secrecy and privacy; of those inner gardens and patios we inherited from the Moors, so nicely hidden in the bosom of each house.

At first I think we can wander about unimpeded. Everything is so exposed, as if offered: front lawns and gardens lead through the two sides of each house to backyards where last minute fencing feels as if it finally occurred to these people that they should have a modicum of privacy somewhere. We do not know, my sister and I, that this apparent availability is not real, that a strict code exists, so pervasive it is never put into words; a code so far-reaching that, for all intents and purposes, no neighbors exist. Contiguous existences are not acknowledged; with few exceptions, no one knows who the next door folks are, what they do or what they think. The exceptions extend only as far as a lukewarm politeness, a greeting with the hand from a distance when the thing is plainly unavoidable.

We are soon warned by Celia not to wander past the invisible fences. She informs our parents who inform us. Our education proceeds on an orderly basis, controlled by a woman who operates from behind curtains and taboos.

Within the boardinghouse it is another matter; Celia doesn't have to worry about Anglo proprieties. The many rooms and suites are full of young people, students from Costa Rica whose radios are busy with Glenn Miller songs that float out of open windows and mix with the honey-collecting frenzy of insects and the constant hum of traffic on Olympic Boulevard, a few houses south. Those young adults, girls I peek at through their partially closed blinds between my room and theirs, and boys studying dentistry into the small hours of the night, are just beginning to fall in love with the strangers they must divorce decades later, when disenchantment forks their road.

In case there is any doubt about the matter, let me repeat: We enter the country on tiptoe, on tenterhooks, when I can pry my fingers off the ship's railing. After an hour with the immigration crew we are not sure whether the grunt of the last one by the door means to go forward or step back, get in the boat or get the hell out of his sight. Father compares him to a German businessman he once knew; Mother says it's simply the aloofness of Anglo-Saxons. I think the airless shack where they do their interrogations, with its barracks-like cleanliness, would do a miner's canary in.

But enough. We pass. My children and my sister's children will flood the country with their singing, but what do we know? Old man Zeledon comes to get us, as I recall now. While the adults renew their lapsed acquaintance (having known each other in Costa Rica when it consisted of a dozen cats), my sister and I stare out the window. At the hugeness, the endless vagary of dwelling humanity. I have come to check it out, to smell it, to be for and against it, to bury my parents, to question God, to flunk trigonometry, to collect signatures for Henry Wallace's Third Party, to answer the telephone and lose my way, in basements of color.

The bad taste the immigration officials leave in our mouths is soon forgotten. The city grows in splendor and logic as we move northeast. Don Luis Zeledon swings past the corner of Wilshire and Western, the busiest intersection in Los Angeles. We are part of an anthill with aqua colored buildings where fat queens of money shake like jello when they laugh. My X-ray vision detects them and makes a note of them; it's not for nothing I am the most politically advanced thirteen-year-old in the world. Didn't I beat up Mario Gonzalez for boasting about Franco two years ago?

Within weeks, I will walk back to Wilshire, attracted by a totally unprecedented Ten Cent store where, for twenty-five cents one can buy cap pistols. Imagine! Within weeks, also, we are put in school. The kids of Wilton Elementary School ignore me totally. They can tell you that without language there is no relationship. My tongue is a deaf-mute in a world where shouting moves the action forward, so all I can do is hang around the edges of the softball diamond. When the teachers force me on one of the sides, I strike out consistently because I have never played the game. Each morning at recess, I am greeted by a chorus of groans.

One boy befriends me. He is slight, wears glasses and has no interest in sports. He is my first friend in the new country, with whom I communicate as best I can. He lives with his mother in a small apartment a block away from Celia's and our friendship consists in my trying to make him gifts of my things and in his refusing to accept them. It works great because we are both loners, losers, prospective bookworms. Then one day he leaves; he and his mother move to another city and I am once again thrown upon my own resources. In school, the boys are still at their endless inning.

Luckily, I discover dust. The newness of everything is full of surprises but these wear out. So what if milk comes in greasy cardboard boxes. So what if Prince Valiant is forever seeking his princess in Sunday's colored landscape. But dust, dust knows everything. Its kingdom is up on the third floor, in the attic. One opens a door, climbs up a narrow set of stairs and there it is, softly everywhere. I have never seen an attic before. This one is not only immense but forbidden, so there is the extra excitement of sneaking up to it. Celia rents the house from an old woman who befriended her and let her move in on condition the family's heirlooms could be stored in the attic. A perfect arrangement. I begin to go through things in that cobwebby light of yesterday. Oh delight. There is dust suspended in the air and dust long dormant on things, like a grey skin. One rubs it off Aladdin's lamp and out come clarinets and photograph albums and quarter inch thick records, shriveled bars of soap, books on farming and on Lincoln Indian head pennies, hats which once flew, drinking flasks, souvenirs of St. Louis. Each item has a story to tell my eyes and hands, and when it's done telling I place it back where it was, story and all, though this last sometimes will not fold up again quite in the same way or fit as snugly as before.

When I know there is no one on the second floor to hear me I play the records on a hand-wound phonograph, a handsome piece of furniture. The Chopin that emerges sounds tinny and militaristic, played fast the way they liked to hear him prior to W.W.I. What is really amusing is that if the machine is not wound fully, the speed runs down and Chopin ends up with the gravelly voice of entropy.

The dust is marvelous small, the leather objects cracked, the papers and documents yellow with defeat. The past of unknown persons has made an attempt to be present here for me, perhaps the last to treat these mementos with sympathy, with wonder and trepidation. The old lady, the sole survivor, will die shortly in the old folks' home for which she has already made arrangements and someone, perhaps Celia, will one day clean out this attic, throwing out everything that cannot be labeled an antique. Out will go the clarinet that has no mouthpiece, the arthritic books, the musty gowns, the distant photographs. Like a tide that fulfills the terms of oblivion, time will sweep aside the record of lives coeval with my grandmother's, and we shall be all a little more ignorant, more orphaned. Not that it can be otherwise. If the past were to accumulate too fully it would suffocate us. But I am not a great defender of the present. I find it wafer thin. And if it doesn't bear the patina of the past, it has no responsible dimension, no human meaning. It is an idiot tick from a clock that upchucks the next same tick as if to feed the never-to-arrive future, that blind owlet happy to never fly.

This grand attic teaches me conservancy. It has the value of smiling sadly, like those portraits of Lincoln I get to know for the first time, features that tell me how wonderful it was that for once the brutal carnage of brother against brother found a voice that didn't rot along with the mangled bodies by the ditch. In the silence of this attic I can sit in a reverie that is not thought, a calm that isn't boredom. I reach out and touch the ghost of another time, compressed into objects that feed the imagination so that they are larger than the time they took to be. I sense the pulse of things that have fully been and are no more, so that I know the same goes for me, that I am young by chance, as it were. And it fills me with awe, this sensation; I am boundlessly amazed and thankful to have it, to know that things cease, that all of what is next is bound to be, totally, and that it will disappear, just as totally, with perhaps a child to wonder at it after discovering a trace of it by chance. Oh long distance! Long road, long and unmanageably manageable journey that thanks God for death because otherwise it would be monstrous and perverse. I am sitting here in a vibrant city, newly arrived and looking for a skeleton key in the hand of a mirror willing to reflect not only light but darkness. Willing to open more doors than I had ever imagined, doors never envisaged by those men in khaki who seemed so reluctant to let us enter.

That is always the paradox of doors. I am coming into my own, myself sometimes only the doorjamb or the knob. Or a shadow moving backwards. But in three years I shall encounter a spider in a dry empty lot across from our house on Fountain Avenue, a spider that lives underground in a tiny hole with a door on top that it can swing open when it chooses. A creature all jump and attention. And I will remember this attic on that day just as much later in my mind's eye I will see my grandmother's tomb on a day of small white clouds and eternity, for I am starting to walk not in a city or a world but in a garden full of connections. The shyness will last decades. I am terrified of telephones and of teachers who have no idea who I am. I want to tell them that all reality is camouflage but the actual words won't be available for another forty years. It doesn't matter in the least. When I sit in this attic, warmer than the hot summer raging outside—for summer has come and I am burning—when I sit quietly surrounded by dust that was once a storm, I am as fulfilled as the odor of geraniums on the dank back patio of my grandmother's house.

I begin. I wind up the phonograph to play Chopin once again but all that he put of Poland or himself in the music is now mine transformed into capricious avenues beneath eucalyptus trees. And California throbs within me with its ocean blues and its stifling canyons, with the wind carrying the odor of sage a puzzled distance.

It's easy to forget where one has been. But I move to be there anyway. Even if the Pericles perishes in mid-Atlantic, sunk by a German torpedo in the middle of a night without fortune on its side, I shall be holding on to its railing and trying the door of those hills that loomed so olively there and so inauspicious. Because we're everywhere we've been, like ghosts dancing next to the molecules the scientists believe in, like dust whirling next to the wind that seems so pure. To hell with time. I am the boy that has no past because I am solid all the way back to the umbilical connection. To see me that way you have to see me in that attic that rebels against itself, an attic that becomes a star and then a galaxy and more, something with the shoulders to hold not just the extinguished flame of a generation but the dust of that skeleton key that opens doors, that manufactures perfume out of nothing, when all the jasmine in the universe has disappeared. It's not a trick for scholars, not a magician's bag. What it is is the truth. In one particular mote of dust I have come to find an American president weeping, and lilacs blooming, and the rhymes of pain. Also photocopies of my darling foot taking the next step, wearing a shoe.

The trap-door spider says, hang onto that railing, boy. Before long I am earning money, sanding cars for a friendly Mexican man a mile away who lives in a house surrounded by sunflowers. I like his daughter, but she is forbidden to come out into the yard where I and some of the college boys from Celia's boardinghouse have found this gold mine. With the money from that and from gardening, my parents take me downtown, to a pawnshop, to purchase a microscope. It is perfectly clear that I am going to become a bacteriologist unless derailed. The derailing comes with the spider days, with reading *Jean Christophe*, with going for music.

Each path along the eucalyptus lanes shuddering in the breeze is mine to follow. But the place I come from is this attic formulated instinctively by the slanting roof, the hot smelling pine boards, the lassitude, the hammock's ataxia. Downstairs, I pound away on an upright piano in the living room, driving everybody crazy, but here, in this prairie of backward glances, with Chopin at the ready, I am the king of rumination. In a way, it's a manger of darkness, a reverse Nativity; the immigration officers are the three wise men; the dust, like an illustrious animal, breathes warmth into my limbs. I am telling you how I was born to speak English, torn away from the corduroy heat of the sugarcane fields. I am telling you the reason why I go round and round in circles, lost, pensive, promising, aromatic, free.

2
THE PERSIMMON DOOR

Celia Valenzuela wasn't too happy to see us go; she had counted on our staying in her boardinghouse at least another six months, which, given her slightly deranged mind, could have meant, or been, forever. But Mother, with her typical spunk, has made the leap and rented a house on Hollywood Boulevard. We are strangely and deliciously on our own in a large, clean house built on the skirts of the hills. The land slopes enough to allow for an apartment below us, in back of the house, an apartment which Mother rents.

Once again in my life everything is utterly new, a breath of pollen transported from the calyx of one flower to another. I have become a teenager, have discovered persimmons in a neighbor's tree and, on the first of January, when I go to the back yard to play, the sky is so blue I have to stop and gape. I can't believe it has turned this pure and cobalt-deep in celebration of the new year, but what else could it be? The earth knows. The sky knows. Armed with the glow of such a sky, each leaf of the grapefruit tree is the greenest it could be. Each leaf of the pepper tree is almost nothing but air pretending chlorophyll. The world is about to begin; it is getting ready to pulse. It might take off. The signs are all around, pulling off the trick of continuity in order to refresh their memories. But also changing minutely with the light: clouds if there are clouds, birds if there are birds.

Things are so new they appear as doors. They open for me; they say whatever first comes into their non-dimensional minds. The freedom they convey gets a bit confused with the anarchy of limitless play. I jump over the fence into the back neighbor's fruit garden and steal a persimmon. I do it astonished at how easy it is to do, how well I get over the wooden fence, how beautiful the garden is, how packed with trees and paths and health, how small the persimmon tree is, how big its leaves are, how large its fruit, how they hang like lanterns the sun has ignited and left burning.

I bite into the persimmon and nobody knows it. The world is just getting started and nobody is watching Eden's fruit. Wheels are only now beginning to touch the ground of experience, judgement is for later. The persimmon tree forgives me, I have lightened its load. And the persimmon itself is made up of slabs of sugar. But oh door, door! You have, always will, an inside and an outside face. The unripened parts of the fruit are surprisingly acrid, enough to tell me I will not steal another one. This is the first glimpse, the entrance to the republic. Everything that comes later hinges upon it.

She's an old woman, this persimmon grower whose world I have invaded. She rents a room in her house with the decorum of a widow who each day dusts the photograph of her husband on the mantelpiece. She comes from the integrity of the past, from perfectly ironed silence, from fresh water and the folded things of time. The minute I taste the acrid flavor of forbidden fruit, my mouth is full of aftershocks, as if I were in the presence of my grandmother.

Lives later, friends will bring Japanese persimmons to the four corners of my tattered life; persimmons that know no acrid parts. Friendship is like that. And when they do I will invariably recall a summer when another persimmon tree, on a steep hillside off Laurel Canyon, glowed with its motherlode of neon lights.

What I am saying is that persimmons glow with eternity's message. Specifically, with the beauty of a moral tone that attaches to them in the most inexplicable manner. By coincidence, as it were; by osmosis. Who knows? Don't forget that for others it has been apples...

But I must stick to chronology, that fly paper of facts: I eat this first and last stolen persimmon in the faint shade of the pepper tree. With mourning doves cooing in the nearby and the opera singer in the dark wooden house to the east of us going up and down La Scala of her throat as if she were the one devouring the fruit.

The sugars dance in my brain, the lesson takes hold in the cat's yellow backroom eye of attention. From thief I go to hunter. Father teaches me to trap doves. All it takes is some feed, a wooden box like the ones vegetables come to market in, a length of string and two short sticks. The feed is placed on the ground under the box which balances on the sticks, one on top of the other. When the doves attempt to feed, they trip the string which connects the box to the sticks. The box comes down and the birds are trapped.

To house these lavender-colored animals with their astonished eyes, I build a wire enclosure beneath the pepper tree. I convince myself that the three doves I catch are happy to be mine even when they neither touch the water nor eat the corn and sunflower seeds I give them. Fortunately, a neighbor reports us. Is it the opera singer from her high balcony of B flats next door? Is it the lady in back who has followed every depraved act of mine since we moved in? An officer from some animal protection agency pays us a visit. He is extremely polite but I have to release the doves. They fly off without rancor.

My father and this officer each follows his own protocol. It is done without the use of much language. The diplomatic pass-port of a consul saves Father from having to pay a fine. It's almost as if we were above the law but the plain fact is that we are dripping with innocence. The man can plainly see that we come from a land where everything is allowed. He advises me to get plain pigeons and tells me where to buy them. I settle down to the pleasurable responsibility of caring for these fat relatives of the thin-necked beauties I had to let go. They turn the mash they eat into song, courtship dances, eggs, and new life. If their wings are limited by wire and their brains by instinct, their cooing knows no barriers.

It must be, is, dazzlingly early. So early one cannot suspect or go beyond it. Everything else crystallizes like honey in its own sweet packaged time. The legality, the sympathy of the law and for the law is, if you can have it, sweet, a new taste. The strange thing will be the discomfort others will exhibit when brought up against my constant sense of surprise, of awe at whatever. As if they didn't feel the same way or it was too painful for some reason to drum up an equal amount of wonder.

They'll find it easier to label me unreasonable, romantic, sentimental or, what is the worst, phoney, when what I'll try to do is share the enviable condition of astonishment. The only thing that makes for brotherhood, incidentally. Let's call it honoring surprise: what I didn't know was religion until no other word worked. The voice at the double edge of things, beyond those who will say, "Oh, persimmons, yes; he goes on so about them!" Meaning to underline their boredom not only with the fruit but with the enthusiasm for natural things per se, for the peculiar solidity and strangeness of things.

I'd like to steal into their souls and rob them of their boredom. Be the thief of what they have no need of. It is precisely at this time that a thief comes to rent a room from us and, while assessing if we have enough to make a real heist worthwhile, he invents that he is an aviator and will fly us to Mexico on a jaunt, for the hell of it. We are so foolish we fall for it. This is the foolishness that keeps us alive and which will never never harm us. The thief gives up and runs off with Father's passport. He is later caught in Oklahoma and spends the war in jail.

On the other hand, our first renters downstairs do the opposite, they need no bars to stay behind them. They survive mostly by collecting coupons for cornflakes, for flour. They are pale, somehow outcast. It's a mother and her son and daughter. Who don't speak, don't mingle. Who suffer from what was back East some tenement disease, an alienation that makes them generate distance, empty space around them.

The boy, the girl, are in their middle and late teens. Both are heavy, sad, silent, always home, perhaps in mourning. There is no sign of a father, or a caress. Their skins are so white they blush under the normal throb of their blood. They belong body and soul to the Depression, to Detroit or Chicago, something as vast as a thousand windows blind with the Sunday afternoon sun of an industrial park. They are in Hollywood now but they have no connection to the yucca plants stabbing the light of the hills with their blades, no response to the yellow grapefruit duplicating suns outside their windows.

The girl says, "Momma, I don't want to go to school today!"

The mother takes a patient's breath, a breath learned in the wards of attrition, and asks why.

"The kids teasing you?"

"The kids are not teasing me, Momma; I just don't want to go to school!"

"They're calling you a Yid, aren't they, Sheila?"

It's like a tragedy intrinsic to their being, to their grandfather having known the distance between Kiev and Lodz on foot, between Lodz and Galveston in the hold of a ship. The boy says something that escapes me. I am only listening because the words come up through the heater vent on the floor of my bedroom, if I haven't fallen asleep. He speaks in a foreign language..... No, wait, he is saying he can't stop eating. So it *is* a foreign language, a construct of fears I am not familiar with. The crying is muffled. He is a fat boy whose mother doesn't want him in her bed because he wets it. She lets him wet his own, cursing the stink.

In the morning, all three are pale again. As if the dark had guaranteed their pink whiteness all over again. When they emerge from the apartment, it is as if they came loose off the laminated door, entering the world sideways, ill at ease, like guilty splinters.

The boy goes on getting fatter; he wants to be made of a gelatinous substance that will quiver. Sheila carries her school books in front of her and stares intently ahead; with crossed arms she traps and tries to flatten out her budding breasts. She doesn't want to exist in the world, Europe has already imprinted itself on her. She is busy erasing herself in every way she knows how. One day I only see half of her. And one day all three disappear, they are gone. Their suitcases and boxes sit on the sidewalk as if abandoned. I am not sure if it's a taxi or a garbage man that finally takes it all away. But when I walk through the empty apartment, their lives are still there. When I touch the skin of the four walls, their misery comes off on my hands. I look out their windows; the trunk of the grapefruit tree is smooth and greenish-grey, like the leg of a pachyderm.

Which is how it gets to feel late at times until I can escape and it is early again, it is my morning and, like water, my life is a simple pouring out of things. Look, the new couple is moving in.

New Yorkers. He says *New Yoork* because that's where he's from, with the electric nervous energy of a handsome thirty-year-old Jew. She's a Bostonian Anglo so she says *New Yawk* though she's trying to say *New Yoork* to make him happy, to be as like him as possible, for they are deliriously in love with one another.

At first, Mother hesitates to rent to them. After all, they are not married yet. But the aura of happiness they exude is too much for her and she stuffs her scruples away in some drawer.

They are here to start a new life, take the film industry by storm, get married and have two children, maybe four. It is going to be a great marriage, one of those that lasts half a century. The moment the apartment is theirs they rush around furnishing it, buying flowers, filling it with answers. We have never seen such happiness in two faces as when they talk and look at each other to see what the words are making their lips do, how they mean to harbor a look in their eyes.

It doesn't last long. She with her fine hair, the future perhaps already caught like a barley seed in her womb. He with the endlessly renewed wanting of her. It ends. We hear it from him as he's packing, desperate to get out of a California that has blown up in his face. Two days before their wedding she's killed trying to cross the Boulevard, near Highland. Someone too clumsy to avoid so much beauty runs over her.

We are left alone, stunned by the little residue of so much that could have been. In the apartment every door is ajar, nobody wants the flavor of opening a cabinet, of fetching a drink, of putting things away. Our footsteps echo obscenely there and, what is that emptiness so early, what is that death with its useless meaning, ricocheting from one wall to another? It's impossibly clear so we don't talk about it. Each of us takes what has happened to that far reach in the hollow inside where only the body can deal with it, in that warehouse where one can set the event down to let it expand the silence.

Oh clouds, you pass overhead moving eastward. We follow you with small greening why's, untasseldly young. I want to record these things that happen to my morning, as it's open-ing. One sees insects like that, a cricket or a spider with a leg missing, no longer able to exult as formidably as when it had its wholeness to trumpet among the weeds. One sees flowers missing a petal, yearling birds in the mouth of Timothy the cat, and damned if it isn't exactly that which underwrites the best of all possible worlds. Any other road is the road of cynics, the folk with the ashen faces. They haven't processed their own deaths enough to admit it.

Yes, she's dead, the blissful unattended bride. She ran across the street. Blinded by delight she saw some homemaker gad-get in the window across and she wanted to bring it home, she saw how it would fit the intricate requirements of breakfast. Our death was there also, waiting for her, where it has always been, giving meaning to everything that has gone before, to the life that ends now, never later.

From our dining room window, where I have gone to count clouds, I count persimmons ripening instead. They are a fence away, a world away. So many; or is it just enough? Figure that one out. The clouds have yet to tell another story.

It is this: an old French couple come to live downstairs. They bring with them the formal pride, the ancient harmonies of a race that has flourished under the king of suns. Father is very pleased to sit outside with the old man who leans on a cane. Together they talk—or wish they could—. They do more than talk. All of Europe, my father's respect and the old man's assurance, are there for them to manifest as presence, by their being together. The old woman busies herself in her kitchen and everyone benefits, I if I am passing by, Mother if it's teatime, my sister who can never say No.

And then, then, Paris falls. With automatic certainty, taking deadly aim, the Germans march into the City of Light, the city they can never own but which they can certainly stain with their boots. They also march into an old man's heart in Los Angeles, they tell him he has no right to catch the morning sun on the brim of his hat any longer and they execute him. He cannot bear to live with the flavor of defeat in his mouth and he dies. He's dead in three days. Weeks later, all in black, his widow returns with a large bouquet of roses for us. The roses perfume our living room for a week. Against that much elegance the Germans can never succeed. But after that we do not rent the apartment again, it becomes a storage area.

Sometimes, when the dust accumulates in the corners, we hear it calling for more dust to come. Dust is the dandruff of existence, the gentle stardust of disintegration falling even on my morning song, as I look past the fence with longing.

In the old woman's yard the persimmons are calling. Each one is meant to be devoured, otherwise it will fall and rot on the ground, among the alarums of the mad green flies opening the door.

3
Dr. Alfaro

He looks like an overripe tomato a child is trying to squeeze for the sake of the explosion. What we suspect is that he uses a girdle, that this girdle gives his shapelessness that dangerous quality, as if everything might blow up at any moment, inundating the flanks of existence with seed. But the truth is that his face goes by the same law of thermodynamics. In this case, his smile plays the role of the inherent girdle on a face which might go the way of all hand grenades. His row of gleaming white teeth exerts its centripetal charms and miraculously and humorously holds the worst from happening.

I don't know how it is that we met him. Probably at Berta Flores' house, which is the hub of the Costa Rican colony in Los Angeles. In 1940 everyone knows everyone else; that is one of the significant differences between the pre-war world and the post-war world. After the war, who the hell knows these new masses parading up and down Hollywood Boulevard? In 1940, even if he doesn't seem middle class, being swarthy enough for a Honduran or a Nicaraguan, and somewhat of a flashy dresser, one (meaning the family) accepts him at face value. But he is definitely a bit too colorful, a bit too amusing, a man in his mid-forties wearing patent leather shoes and a diamond ring on one of his fingers. It is only because we live three thousand miles away from home and feel that we have to stick together that we accept him in our house and take to him.

He started coming to visit after we had left Celia's boardinghouse and had our very own house, on Hollywood Boulevard, between La Brea and Fairfax. He comes singly or with his fiance, a florid blonde who adores him and who, because she's American and delicious-looking, gives him all the credibility he needs.

Elvira, though large, has even features and fine skin. She is attractive the way a large milkshake might be attractive, or if one goes exclusively by one's gonads. Together, Dr. Alfaro and Elvira form a strange and ludicrous couple: She the sleeping goddess of flesh and he the short brown dandy with the slicked down hair and the maraca smile (with gold fillings to go with the diamond ring).

He is fun to listen to because he tells such tall tales. He loves to boast of past exploits and of encounters with the great of the earth. The list includes Mussolini, with whom he claims to have eaten spaghetti.

Such stories are told to the undisguised laughter of my father, who eggs him on to tell us more absurdities. Dr. Alfaro always complies. It doesn't matter how patently untrue or unbelievable the stories are. He either does not take our reactions at face value or does not care. I believe that in some way he sees himself as the necessary buffoon, bringing a bit of absurdity into our lives. It does not matter that it is at his expense; the sparkle is the thing. He doesn't appear to suffer playing the clown, he thoroughly enjoys himself and gets lost in the telling of things. Again, perhaps it is all done for the sake of Elvira, who doesn't understand but sees us hanging on to every word and who, when we laugh, assumes we are laughing with him, not at him. Or he may need our affection at all cost and believes he's getting it. Sometimes I suspect he knows that we see him as this beached whale who spouts off as if he were in mid-ocean. At such times I think he prefers to be a whale than the minnow he must be elsewhere; where he works, for instance.

He is so unmitigatingly nothing, so unlimitedly empty, so needy, and yet so voluptuously accompanied by this woman who can sit silent for hours listening to us converse in Spanish, that we suspend our disbelief and listen to him. More often than not, besides the potato chips and the wine, my parents provide music or he brings some of his own records. We ask him to dance with his disparate woman and then this clumsy mass of flesh rises to the occasion. It is marvelous to watch. He leads his willing, swooning mate through all the popular Latin dances of the day in such a smooth and competent if not blatant manner that one has the clear choice of watching in wonder or laughing hysterically. And, in either case, the reaction is right.

This is the astounding key to this personage who can discuss neither politics nor history nor philosophy, who professes no religion, knows nothing of art, eschews sports, reads nothing, not even the paper, and who suspects nothing. He isn't filled with wonder, does not know how to step out of line, has nothing but stuffing between his front and back, elicits no signs of revelation, stature or enlightenment and, when cornered, cannot tell you how to cure a cold. He is extraordinarily empty, with the unfrayed ego of a buffoon bouncing in his innards, to the amusement of those who hear the bumps.

Within that vast territory of blandness, he moves (he certainly dances) with a kind of splendor that lends him half a measure of respect. It also provides him with half a portion of derision. His dancing includes both halves of the equation. It is an accomplishment but an accomplishment well within the province of banality. It makes sense that he should be adept at something falling within the scope of the mundane, the innocuous, shambling through life without more purpose than to be able to flash momentarily like a bit of mica aslant in a field.

But let us say that he has perfected the abandon with which he dances. In another man, a half-way handsome man, this kind of thing would bring only admiration. With Dr. Alfaro, given the figure he cuts, no admiration is possible without its share of ridicule. Again, he must know this and not care, or he sees it as the necessary concomitant to the applause he has to have. One thing is certain, if he feels pain he never shows it. Our laughter must convey less malice than it does joy. The fact is that the more we laugh the more he gives of himself, the more he exerts himself. The blank blonde is like a hosannah in his arms, a somnambulist awash in proximity, in a constant impending climax with her half-closed eyes, body well pressed against his, going where he hurls her in a swirl of extremities and not so accidentally returning to the grind and rub again.

We sit and watch, I with my mouth open, knowing someday I am going to have to learn how to swim in female seas, and drown for all I care. Dr. Alfaro doesn't come too often; once a week at the most, sometimes only twice a month. My life meantime is an exploration of totally different things, of the tops of trees, which I love to climb; of the neighboring avocado orchard; of the bottle-brush tree in the empty lot across the boulevard, with its seedpods like possible pipe bowls for the tobacco I dream of stealing from Father; of the plum tree two blocks away in another empty lot between two magnificent houses; of the languid pepper tree in our own backyard and of the grapefruit tree where the moods of sun and cloud translate into solitude and olfactory mysteries somehow essential to my being; of the hills a few blocks away, the mesquite and manzanita bushes garlanded in golden parasitic growth; of the dry heat of those hills, formula for my specific existence.

These parties my parents give, when Dr. Alfaro and his woman come, are the premature and abrupt dance of humanity parading before me, interrupting with too much naked light the fogbanks where my states of being are being formed. They are moments when I can see what it will mean to be a part of a troop of bipeds. This Dr. Alfaro comes and goes, wearing the monkey suit of his person, being willing to entertain and masturbate in front of us like a chimpanzee, which he resembles to a remarkable degree. Albeit a chimp dragging along a prize butterfly discovered among the brown brick buildings on the west edge of downtown, where each apartment complex houses within it something stunted and relocated about man, something reduced to the hum of a refrigerator, the pale circumference of a lamp, threadbare rugs and the footsteps of ghostly lives in the hallways. She comes from there, she lives in a nondescript building foreign to song and effort, among garages and storefront groceries selling rancid butter and stale cornflakes.

They come this far to dance for us. He to tell us his tall tales and she to lie languorously on the sofa with her soft chocolate eyes, the two of them feeding on potato chips of no importance, on wine of no transcendence, on what they need of friendship because they hear us talking about Cervantes and suspect he's more than a name, they hear Father talk about the seas of the moon and wonder if we don't possess life everlasting, they see Mother's torn fingers after a day in a garment factory and can tell that we mean to break away from circumstance. Contact with us makes them real; they can go home and make love again, they can go home and check their eyebrows in the mirror, surprised at how they move again, I don't know…

He could be an orderly in some hospital. The doctor business is pure fantasy. Perhaps he sells prosthetic devices to the medical profession. We have never inquired where he works. He turns into a doctor the minute he walks out the door after his shift pulling bedpans out from under emaciated behinds, the second he turns his sales slips in to the fat-jowled distributor. Calling himself a doctor is all he needs to wear as badge in order to dance for us with his beautiful doll.

He can never be alone. That is the price he has to pay. Never alone to allow a single questioning voice to arise. If such a thing were to happen there would be an immediate implosion and he would cease to exist. The sham extends to the border towns where death checks your papers. It's serious. That is why the fact that he lives alone is so spectacular. I wish someone could tell me how he does it.

He cannot live with Elvira, he doesn't know a thing about relationship. It takes time each day to put on the make-up and what would she say? But he avoids solitude, he has ways to buttress the space around him with cotton, he goes on a million errands, for vaporub, for the unread newspaper, for peanuts, for the cigarettes that stain the fat of two fingers, for the nail polish he likes to use on his toenails. He has a car which goes with him on errands to the edge of purity, across and around the city, over cobblestones and the oily pavement of major boulevards sadly in need of sense. His car is another badge. The devil says that when he has Elvira in the front seat his right hand looks for elves in her triangular forest.

In that car, minimal with privacy, he takes us to the beach. In Santa Monica or Venice, the contrast between his roly poly body, drenched in drugstore cologne, and the white odalisqueness of his companion is simply tremendous, something people point to. He is this strident syrup pouring itself over her cool slices of moonlight, fretting over her, getting her ices. It is a festive time but why he has to wear a Mexican hat is anybody's guess. People stare. I go a few hundred feet away and find myself a spot in the sand near the waves, alone, ashamed for him.

December starts and never ends. The Japanese savage Pearl Harbor and war begins. Fearing an attack on Los Angeles, we pack and go to Mexico City for six months, see that life there is impossible, and return with our tails between our legs. Dr. Alfaro finds an apartment for us in, of all places, the west side of downtown, to which we must adjust. I do it by becoming a mole, by reading Charles Darwin and books about submarine warfare, catching cold during gym class because all I do is stand in my shorts doing nothing while the rest of the class pretends a rubber ball is important. What a miserable time!

He takes us out to Venice Beach and in the cotton candy afternoon haze and pack of humanity we see a newspaper headline with photos of an upside down Mussolini. Dr. Alfaro pretends sadness. My father turns into Garibaldi, to be controlled by Mother who adroitly points out to him that we don't have the money to get home on the trolley. What a farce history can be! We settle for hotdogs and forget those violenced bodies dank in newspaper ink. These are the medicinal attitudes: Youth, prejudice, fantasy and indifference. The blond woman is munching on caramel popcorn and the afternoon, pregnant with history and fading rapidly, sinks near us into the murky misanthropic waters. At home we get rid of the last bits of sand from between our toes, the last rasping echo from the beaks of the low-flying seagulls and shower, taking to bed the salt water buffeting which the doctor claims to be healthy.

In one of those other grey buildings near us, perhaps within shouting distance, in one of the apartments chosen by narrow hallways to be dark with darkness, our good friend plunges into the ever golden flesh of his sunflower so let me recap. At thirteen and buried in my various ivory tunnels, the crests of trees, the gorgeous foreign landscape, the school where language is the usual barrier, Dr. Alfaro is the peripheral clown figure whose shadow makes a dent in my sexuality. He is the superb anti-role model, the Latin asshole licking the boots of America and getting away with murder.

Fifty years later, as the birds of memory fly, one can see him coming and going, busy with shit. One day he disappears. Is it into a vacant lot perhaps? You ask me what kind of car he drives and I'll tell you : a shiny beetle. The guy is kind, he gives me a dollar camera and I shoot him. He is perspicacious when he has to squirm. The best thing about him is that he isn't proud. He is not quick either but you can't have everything. He is warm. If you touch him you will discover this. Warm, like blubber, and expansive, like asphalt on a warm day, vain like a loud necktie, silly like a waddling duck. I tell you he dances as if he were an attractive male item, placing certain items of his anatomy in front of you in the manner of a fluid totem pole. His soul oozes out the sides of his corset like a great ness of jello and you would think this would come to an end but no, because, like all things shallow, operettas, five and tens, exploratory operations, the shallow never knows how to end.

One wonders where he is now, if alive. Where buried if dead. I'd say he's still in the middle of a lifetime of mediocre thinking, breathing, eating, drinking; in the midst of an eternity of mediocre jobs, mediocre clothes, mediocre eyesight and the mediocre abusing of a love affair fast going nowhere. That's where he is. These things don't end easily. It involves a strength I know nothing about. I can despise him but I can no longer feel condescending towards him. I find the means by which to pay him homage, this brilliant non-entity with his patent leather shoes, his brown stripe suit, his flowing tie, his slicked-down hair, his inability to think, his gorgeous female, his inventiveness, his unacknowledged desolation, his buried origins, his murky future, his tepid dreams, his wanting to be loved, his deodorant and his shaving cream.

No matter who we are we are no different. When I see that it's time to put out the light and that all lives are lived for their own recognizable shape, then I go back to the drawing table where this figure has been pinned down like a butterfly and I don't ask him how he informed his sense of self, I salute him for dancing for a while, I celebrate his undignified version of commitment, I applaud his vulgar skies, his armpits, his standard vocabulary, his wallet, the thinness of his gifts, the way he must have said good-bye to Elvira one day when he turned the faithfulness of her odor, her abundance, her half-closed eyes, into enough. I have lived to explore meaningless directions; I have sung the shape of the pear and the veins of the stallion just as he has lived within the closed circuitry of eliding seconds, masses of them, conventional and lacking in style, hurtling towards the funeral another million seconds give him at the time of his discolored death. Oh lost, credulous, satisfied, mistaken, unabused, illogical, inconsequential, boring man; man of easy dirt, easy clean, easy gullet, easy payment, easy ailments, easy nurses and priests and acquaintances like ourselves, laughing, talking behind his back, c'mon, imitating his posturings, asking him to kiss her, watching the lingering kisses he gives her upon our request so that we can be slightly scandalized and for which she lowers her large eyelids, her splendid lashes, the better to give him her soul, her tongue, her largely puzzled love.

I place him on the balance. My words are fulcrum enough if you can believe his preposterousness is no more invalid than burning, hankering to sing. I'd give anything to know what has become of this cipher, this dancing shadow whom the neighbors heard laughing loudly during those pathetic parties. Such an improper carcass! Such a tropical *cholo!* Brother of inconsequence, of the days of the week and of the Virgin Mary, who must have had his own morning glory childhood, his sweet armrest mother, her nipples, his opening, a first indigo pain, a paternal kissing cousin, napkins under the chin, an elevator shoe, visits to someone in the country, tears of rage. He entertained us when we were so young we thought ourselves superior and, while dying somewhere of something quirky and sad, allowed us our laugh.

Since your time, oh doctor of appearances, I have met one or two other persons almost like you, equally without substance, equally mellifluous and unguarded and absurd. But you take the cake, beloved shadow, you place thirteen candles on it and tell me I win, I am your better and, behind my back, your successor. Oh yes, you say quite openly to my face that I am your survivor but I know what you think, when you think.

I dance when drunk. I paint when frightened. I write when angels piss, disfiguring my alphabet of dung. You danced, you loved and adored something like the queen of all surrounding vegetation. What was it? Tell me how you lived without crutches, delighting in appearances! Your adoration was the perfect thing.

Will you show me how to adore?

As a boy, in my newness, I see you in my life as a blessing. Now, opaque and unquiet, I see you mirroring a vast and terrible emptiness. You are like plain, foolish water; not the water of rivers or rain, let alone the lion mane of ocean spray, but water, still water, water in a glass that looks up humbly to reflect me after all is said and done and which, because my hand trembles, does a little jig with my face and converts me to your ways, to your inept, quicksilver clowning.

4
BETTY CROFT

On the first day of creation, with Botticelli and the initial goddess of sensuality in collusion, I am ushered into the classroom, but don't see her. It takes days before she emerges from that child-soup of thirty odd faces. Then I know what the inevitable is all about.

When I am first brought in I sit down where the teacher assigns me and keep my eyes down. She and the rest of the imps are singing Santa Maria with true Neapolitan fervor to please the authorities but everyone is really checking me out, poking each other with repressed laughter at the specimen that has landed in their midst.

But the inevitable doesn't take long to manifest itself; I see her, as if shining among shadows. She sits across the room and all I learn is how to look at her. Then the Chinese fortune cookie opens up of its own accord; the teacher calls for volunteers to help me with reading and she raises her hand. Because she is the most curious; because she has already caught me looking at her and has smiled her nearly oriental smile.

The remedial reading is done in a separate classroom where there are just the two of us and the ubiquitous American flag. It's where we have to sit close to each other in order to tackle those unpronounceable W's as in 'wood' and 'want.'

Because I had already graduated from the sixth grade, in Costa Rica, I was bitter about having to repeat the grade just to pick up some English. It had seemed ignominious. But now I am instantly converted to this wisdom of keeping me back. And may the English language take forever in pouring into my brain when what it comes to be eventually (Shakespeare, Blake, Tom McGrath) are her lips inches away from my ears.

My grandmother, when we knew for certain we were leaving for the States, gathered me and my sister each afternoon and began the task. I remember thinking, with the first few words she taught us,—all right, I know eight, now ten, tomorrow twelve—but how am I going to learn thousands, tens of thousands? And the unphonetic quandaries, the difficult pronunciations, the dozen uses of such an innocent-looking item as the word 'by.'

We'd be sitting in the corridor next to the ferns of the patio, on our wicker chairs and my mind would wander off, looking at the Dutch tapestry on the wall, with its windmill and ducks by a canal, convinced that I'd never get to those words in English. I didn't know that the brain learns exponentially. I didn't know that one day a grandmother would be replaced by a girl with the springtime English of a twelve-year-old.

She is also a shaft of sunlight flooding the room; something playful, kittenish, instantly my perfect opposite and my terrible taskmaster. Suspended chalk dust in the air catches milkfire and one would think she would make me speak without a fault but it doesn't work that way. In the amperage of that room so electrically ours I still stumble over sounds the Spanish language never prepared me for and which my beloved grandmother, in her last-minute attempt to teach me a little

English, never emphasized. I keep saying 'gud' for 'wood' while she shakes her head in dismay.

"No! Don't say 'gud' with a G. It's with a W! See? Watch my lips."

I watch. If I were a camera I'd be shooting a close-up of two petals as they unfold in a speeded up time sequence. They are in sync and they are perfumed.

When it is my turn to imitate the sound, it doesn't work.

"Put your lips together, silly! Pucker up!" With her hand she squeezes the sides of my mouth and I pretend she's hurting me. It's a hands-on lesson that goes far beyond what I have to learn; it's what I want to learn. She seems able to touch me without a problem whereas I am incapacitated for any coordinated movement, especially of my mouth. Since puckering the lips is not part of the Spanish architecture of the mouth, I remain stuck on 'gud.' And even if I was stupid enough to want to get over this hurdle and thus lose the chance to watch her lips at close range, I can't manage that almost non-existent sound that adheres itself to the following vowel. Because what the English W wants to be is a kiss and all I can do is wish I knew enough to tell her this, to see what she'd say. Kissing is the way she could teach me how to pronounce a W perfectly; her lips and mine could agree on it without a hitch then. But a kiss is out of reach.

The full sentence she wants me to say is, 'In the wood the birds are singing.' Once again it comes out, 'In the gud the birds are singing,' so she slaps my hand playfully.

"Listen! Pucker up then open the lips. Watch me!" She purses her lips once again and says the perfect word. "See? It's nothing...."

But the duck goes on pronouncing 'gud,' 'gud.'

She pretends to lose her temper, which makes her more adorable than ever. I have wasted more than a decade of my life without the benefit of an embraceable girlish storm.

"Are you dumb?" she asks. "You must be dumb!"

A tiny devil plops into the crook of my ear and sneers. "Say, fellow, do us a favor" he says. "If this girl starts to think you are dumb, really dumb, it will be over. Do you really want that?"

Devils have a way of plunging one into icy water. "So what do I do?" I ask shivering, "you know I can't pronounce that word…"

"Try turning the tables around. You know how these Anglos stumble over the Spanish R's. Put her to the test. There's no time to lose! Soon she won't want to spend those endless afternoons with you in the playground!"

He's right. I snap shut the reading manual and look her straight in the eye. "I teach you Spanish, show you dumb!" I say in my best pidgin English.

She is caught off guard. "Spanish?" Spanish is easy, her eyes say. "Sure, why not?"

"All right! Look to my lips! Say 'girasol'." I pronounce the word slowly, as if the sunflower that it is was rounding out its day in the mouth of the sun.

What she says is 'jirrasoul' and I laugh. It's an important victory.

In the playground, after school, where she has to remain because her mother (who works at the dry cleaning establishment across the street) gets off at four, she and I play so much on the jungle jim and the sandboxes beneath the venerable pepper trees that not even a lifetime of drudgery will erase the wonder of it, that sweet, extravagant being one when we're two. She and I, almost alone on that yard, never stop emptying ourselves into the other. We are like those small yellow field moths, weeds that have learned to fly in circles around each other as if pollinating space. The only time I can be happy is when I am with her, and then it's on the verge of not being that but a remarkable and curious hurt. The other times, alone, with the family, with Stormy, the boy who lives around the corner from my house, down Sierra Bonita Avenue, everything is a waiting, without significance. And it's then that one gets to doubting. Does she think of me? Does she know how I feel about her?

In this one-dimensional, cardboard-stiff world, I fight against doubt with very few weapons. Memory is one. A smile two days ago. The fight over a cookie, she grabbing me and taking the cookie away. Cheating with memory, exaggerating, daydreaming are other weapons. Daydreaming has the advantage of consuming large chunks of time when not with her.

During the aberrant weekends, Stormy and I climb the hills. He is a nice enough boy, with as many freckles as his father has supersweet grapes in his backyard, but I am with him only to make the time pass a little faster. One day, up in Laurel Canyon, we discover a waterfall and the pool of water it has carved for itself. We jump in to cool ourselves and I am my old self. What a simple comfort that is! But it doesn't last very long; it's as if a snake were to crawl into its old skin. 'I am home,' it might think, but home has cracked wide open and the snake spills out. I spill out onto the thought of her, the hankering for the glow of her skin.

And as if her skin were not enough, there's the rest of her with the body of a girl before she knows it, lean, hungry for play, happy to fly. Her brown wavy hair is long enough for her to have to toss it aside now and then, with that gesture that is so feminine. Best of all is her face, with the skin tightly drawn over cheeks and forehead, and the supremacy of light that frames her eyes. And the world there, mirthful, mischievous, deep as elegance. World beyond which her soul is implicated in harmonies. Ah, Betty Croft, gingham-dressed with bows and shining shoes as we play in the dawn's early light of so much to come! What do we know? We know everything, the potential, the best of flavors.

When I get home, after canceling time and space with her, I eat some soda crackers, drink a glass of sugar water and go climb the pepper tree in the backyard. The grapefruit tree is too difficult and dark but the pepper tree leans down to hoist one up and it has airy branches. On one branch—our branch— I have carved our initials. And I go over the day. If by an improbable hint she has told me she is going to share nothing else than eternity with me, if she has smiled when she wasn't even there, if she has misbehaved and the teacher has had to speak to her as if she had the right, I pour over the details. I see us sitting together while I mispronounce everything on purpose, I in disarray and she with her body carelessly on the seat, light as a scarf.

Once in a while, the teacher replaces her with another girl. Who knows, perhaps she thinks I am in love with her. How ignorant can a person get. As if I wasn't already way beyond, in uncharted territory.

Becky is tall, blond, pretty, but she might as well be a rock. With her an hour is like the hour I have to spend each Sunday at Mass, something interminable and unproductive. But Betty likes her so I am nice to her. If Becky knew Spanish I would pin her down and have her tell me what that glance was the two of them exchanged the other day just as the class was lining up for recess in the hall and Becky and I came out of the remedial room. Betty raised her chin as if asking something and Becky nodded, smiling.

Maybe it's just that all other boys, being used to having girls around them all the time, don't pay any attention. They take girls for granted. They don't realize how privileged they are, they have not caught on to those subtle differences starting to show now and blissfully ignore the sexual locomotive hurtling toward them at a hundred miles an hour.

What has made her and Becky curious may be my alertness, my pleasure in being in their company. I come from six years in an all-boys' school so her proximity is immense. In Costa Rica the educational system wisely keeps boys and girls apart in different schools. For their postponed delight. Consequently, for me, sitting next to the girl, watching her lips, catching that fragrance that is headier than any perfume, is tantamount to a taboo.

There is a perfume, a dream odor to a girl's body, that boys don't have. It was the first thing I noticed when she and I were allowed to sit next to each other. I had already seen her form, her dancing spirit from across the classroom, but catching that fragrance when she was inches from me was different. Like the toss of her head, to keep her hair off her face, it was something so feminine and foreign that it taught me more English than any textbook could have done.

When she stood before me, at close range, everything changed. Small as she was she brought the charm of the English language in her hands. It was dawn. A dawn so clean, so pure, so unmistakable that at first I thought all things would be radiance from then on. She caused me to feel like an ivory moon reflecting that dawn. The desire to learn was the desire to be her, to go on foraging in that light that was threshold, formless invitation. There was only one thing to understand, out of which all subsequent understanding derives, and that is how alive one feels with desire, how quick it is to follow someone without having the flame scorch the garment of flesh. A dancing as in her eyes. I have begun to dance, deeply, in the center of a choir of thanks. Because of her, it might be possible to sparkle, to shine. Consciousness has taken hold of the world she offers me; the old garden has benignly retreated a fraction of a self away to make room for states of being that few can hint at.

Ferris wheel me, flower-softened cliff girl. She runs toward me, a chain link fence between us, and I see her as pattern and solar hum. I am in plain sight of her to be morning after the child's catnap, pirouette of darkness falling into the sweet hay of balking gravities. Love with her is love, even if we never say it, can't, me with my attempts at English and she with her inscrutable girlish modesty. Even if we run circles around each other, and hover over the honey melon blossoms of doubt and certainty. The yes petals saying no and the no petals muttering perhaps, perhaps.

It's not so strange that I know nothing about her. How can I know anything when I know nothing about myself? But if one were to look inside my breast, one would find a surprising largeness has opened a store there for her shopping convenience. "Come in and take what you need. That Virgin doing cartwheels, for instance, product of my having stared at all the statues of the Virgin Mary in church, she's a Shirley Temple doll, silk bloomers and all. Take her. She'll improve the madrepore skills of your growth, she'll assure you I am only an annunciation, a madrigal.

"She's only a small gift. The bargain is me. Take me with you everywhere, like a postage stamp glued to yourself. Mail me to your life. On the envelope of your girl's body. Then you can go anywhere and I will validate you. I'll add color to the addresses you will visit in the years to come."

Because one day school is over. The page turns. I have not worried about this. I have not understood that she will go to the seventh grade God knows where and I will be placed in the ninth grade at Fairfax High School, miles away to go on foot. With the suddenness of a nightmare the teacher disappears, the hundreds of kids melt away, the metal gates at the playground entrance clang shut and are padlocked and she, Betty Croft, who was my water and my air and wafer and light of day, she is gone. She is no more. An infinite summer of brutal heat descends upon my landscape, on the million hours that digest each other like enormous snails, one devouring the next, endlessly.

I climb the pepper tree and pretend to play the aviator, as I've always done, this time imitating the roar of the motor with my mouth to disguise another noise. The breeze moves the tiny leaves of the tree, it wants to shake the small red pods loaded with seed into producing a little music but I fly nowhere in the silence of the vacuumed day.

A ladybug who investigates my fingernail lifts its Volkswagen hood, exposes its inexpensive black wings and flies off into the upper reaches of the pepper tree. The little aviator has said something like 'nothing is real,' nothing that boils in the skull anyway.

In the house, Father is working on an article for a Costa Rican newspaper on his Spanish typewriter. I hear the fast pecking of two fingers on the twenty-six odd signs and flinch when I recall there's no W on that machine. 'Madera' is what he will write if he wants to talk about the wood in a lumbershop and 'bosque' if he wants to refer to the timber line below Mount Wilson. "You have taken the word 'wood' with you, Betty Croft. Perhaps when you use it you will be reminded of the Spanish boy you knew in the sixth grade, who couldn't pronounce it right. The boy who, once, in the playground, tried his best to tell you that he liked you and made such a mess of the sentence it wasn't understood. Yes, even if afterwards, all his English will claim you and his grandmother as its seed."

The past is gone. As is the future. For it is just as worthless. I no longer bank on it. Even if once, six years later, I am standing at the corner of Hollywood and Vine waiting for a bus to take me home to my basement apartment in the hills and I see her in the crowd. Who else could it be with that taut skin over the slightly prominent cheekbones? Whose the radiance but hers? At that instant my heart turns into the impassable barrier. She is with two other girls and I hesitate.

To be with her again so suddenly would be pure chaos. My hands and knees are jelly. What words could I say to her in such a state? I am no Chaplin who has given her her sight, I am his nameless clone chewing on an anonymous flower. I let her go. She boards a bus with her friends, oblivious to my presence, and I lose her forever.

5
PEARL HARBOR SO SMALL

One of Mother's roomers, a fellow who is forever vowing to join the French army and fight against Adolf Hitler, volunteers instead to take me to Fairfax High School, where they have a ninth grade, and convince the administration to enroll me. I know enough English now and why not, I'll only be a year younger than my classmates.

The only problem is that I am physically so small. In elementary school I was always at the end of the line, fighting with Mario Gonzalez for second place. And once, when my parents ran into me unexpectedly in a street in San Jose, they were appalled to see that the little runt they had seen walking toward them was their own flesh and blood. Maybe they thought that by telling me they were worried I would straighten out but all they managed to do was fill me with the notion that I had a condition that wasn't likely to change.

When Frank and I arrive at Fairfax High the first day, with crowds of students all over the front lawn, some senior lettermen standing by a hedge of giant bamboo look at me with open-mouthed astonishment and Frank, this great future fighter for democracy, grins when they drop a remark that escapes my burning ears.

But it doesn't matter, humiliation is something that one learns to swallow. Eventually, I put on a few more inches. And I steer clear of lettermen, of football and other ludicrous sports that are none of my business. Besides, what takes place during this ambiguous year has to do with other, very different things.

In the library upstairs, where new students are being enrolled and where I continue to be the object of everyone's surprise, Frank convinces the authorities that I am ready for the ninth grade. He's quite a handsome man and what forty-year-old woman wearing bifocals for better vision is going to resist this fellow who smiles at her as if she were Vivian Leigh? I am in.

For months I walk the halls fearing that a bully is going to grab me and stuff me into a locker. According to the rumor-mongers, short guys like myself who whisper these things out of the side of their mouths and are never seen again, hazing is not unknown in the school. But it never happens. The only indignity I suffer takes place after gym class one day when a whole group of us has just showered and is toweling off. A big guy flicks me with his towel. The pain makes me furious. I leap at him and he just pushes me away as if I were a bug.

When I try to pick fights with boys more my size, I am left with the feeling that I have merely managed to prove the wrong thing. The truth is, there is not a single interesting boy, not a soul in school, as far as I can see, with my lonely energies. Everyone is so distant he could be a Martian, and the girls are even more removed from possibility. They could be Jupiterians. Because they pretend to be women, as some of them already are, they are inconceivably distant; when they hover around one of the tall, mature boys in the halls, I feel something like repulsion towards them. Instead of realizing that someday I might be tall and fluent enough in English to attract their attention, it comes home to me that I am a freak. In the mirror I see an insignificant kid with black, curly hair destined for a lighthouse position offshore somewhere bleak and weather-beaten. One by one the childhood candles go out, with only the wax dripping down to basement cores of rec-ollection.

More important than school is the walk I must take every morning to get there and, in the afternoon, the walk home. Perhaps four miles all told. Part of it cuts diagonally through Hollywood, following the streetcar tracks that swing down from Hollywood Boulevard at La Brea and which cross Fairfax Avenue at Santa Monica Boulevard. Half my walk is down residential streets and half following the tracks. The tracks are my only source of learning, my only education. The unindelible attempts teachers make to teach me anything at Fairfax come to nothing; I retain absolutely nothing, no memory of a significant text, of an inspired counselor, nothing. The teachers could be replaced by dead bodies; at least dead bodies would hold the interest of the class without having to go through the pretense that something is happening.

My single, true teacher is this double line of steel tracks held up by the half-submerged wooden ties that will smell of creosote till the end of time. On those tracks I learn balance, a minor game consisting of trying to stay on the three-inch rail as long as I can. The game doesn't defeat boredom. And it is when boredom becomes unbearable that the riddle appears. Much later I learn such a thing is called a paradox. For me it is a riddle pure and simple, but one which undermines the little nest of logic I have been trying to build under my feet. The riddle is this: Why, if the two rails are parallel, set that way so that the red streetcars can ride on them with their huge wheels, why do the two rails merge in the near horizon, some five or six blocks away?

Sure, I can blame the eye too, and get out of the difficulty. Ordinary people do just that and get to live long and fruitful lives without bothering with such trifles. One makes the decision that it's a trick of the eye and, presto, no problem. But if you like to scratch an itch even if you know it's going to itch more, you know you cannot blame one, two or three eyes. Or the brain, for that matter. The problem is real: Here are two rails running parallel to one another all the time, here and there and far away. But they blur into one in the distance. To say that that is the nature of distance would be like saying that air is made up of oxygen and hydrogen. What are oxygen and hydrogen? Elements? Then what are elements?

Distance is a paradox. Or perhaps the parallel lines we follow to get to it are the paradox. With time, as we move on and on down the tracks, we enjoy the company of those parallel lines and the luxury of their ever receding fusion where we can never be. Being at the point of union cannot take place just as there is no actual union. Could one say: because there is no actual union? We can only be among the honest but humdrum separation implicit in parallelism.

Or I count ties. The ties are invitations to stop, to pause on one's way, and counting them is a way of choosing not to stop, forsaking the particulars of a particular space. It involves regret because those ties are there for me when nothing else is. So numbers are a form of regret, no matter how abstract they are. Math is the highest form of sentimentality.

That sun-weathered stretch of track I must traverse and return with and by is an endless ladder laid down for me so I can climb nowhere. In school they talk about climbing, about goals and ambition, but it all seems false, a thirst housed in mediocrity. My riddle has already taught me one can never reach that point so beckoning a mixture of horizon and desire. And so it is with pleasure that at lunch time I retreat to the sunken garden at the northwest corner of the school. There, the bright roundness of berries and the perfect roses can tell me how a core of concentration can unfold. How a fist becomes a handshake. It is a small but formal garden, with paths bordered by boxwood hedges, trees providing shade and silence. Why it is there and why nobody likes it is a mystery. It will eventually give way to another building where nothing is taught, where experts make sure brain connections are replaced by spiderwebs.

Just a few years before I was the enthusiast who would organize morning expeditions to go and walk our teacher Rosita Font to school. Learning then was an adventure, a flying out the window with wonder because there was a caring for each of us fledglings. At Fairfax the undistinguished boredom hangs like a cloud no wind can send away; the teachers have fallen into the trough of each textbook, and from those depths they hold forth endlessly with dreary, monotone voices. These are teachers who don't want to get the students excited about anything, certainly not about the 5,000 years man has been mischievously poking around among the stars and the mushroom-studded meadows, the blue waves of the seven seas, and the Shakespearean depths of the human heart.

I have even lost the benefit of my father's small library. All those books were left behind in Costa Rica: Madame Blavatsky and the *Popol Vuh*, *Juventud en Cruz*, the terrifying memoirs of a French boy tortured by his mother, the mystical writings of Mario Luna, the Stendhal I was too young to read....

What I have is the endless sun beating down upon me in the afternoons on the way home, filtering down through a smog strong enough at times to make my eyes water. But better these rails pirouetting sedately away into their puzzling unison, unison where the world boils down to trillions of naked horrors, than the pap they dish out in this public school.

I am forever merely walking, swinging left arm to right leg, right arm to left leg, wearing pair after pair of shoes out. In Costa Rica we had accompanied our teachers to school floating several inches off the ground, five or six of us sixth graders like butterflies hovering around her, heading for the beloved school past the Otoya neighborhood with its palms and cork trees, through the palpitating brightness of an endless summer weather world, so shoes never wore out. The school itself was so special one could not help but want to be in it. It had been designed and brought over from Belgium at the turn of the century, metal plate by metal plate, for it was all made of steel. It was a whole block long and two stories high, with inner courtyards of stone, and it was surrounded by a network of playgrounds that masqueraded as parks. At Fairfax High all this has shrunk to the sunken garden where I spend my lunch hour. One corner of shuddering roses and the rest a hundred thousand bricks that promise to shrink your brain to the size of a conventional citizen.

But walking the rails I shed all the idiocy and endlessness of the school day. The earth is flatly round now. I am an ant beneath the flat iron sun, under the dispensation of an un-equivocal nothingness, a nothingness that doesn't come dressed in the vulgar trappings of education. I walk and walk. I wear my shoes out counting the tens of thousands of steps I take. And then a war stops me in my tracks.

The date, inconsequential for most of the day, is December 7, 1941. In the afternoon, on the way home, I pass a newspaper vending machine. The Examiner is soaked in black ink, the headline implicitly containing thousands of lives in the bal-ance. I, who don't know where Pearl Harbor is, except that, of course, it is beyond where my two rails meet, am faintly alarmed that it should have been attacked. But when, just about home, I run into our neighbors, the persimmon lady and her boarder, and tell them the news, I know what has happened: We, all of us, my folks and the people down the street, are in imminent danger. From something as awkward and hairy as a tarantula.

War is no longer talk. We are in danger of losing our lives, of not hearing the ice cream truck go by after dinner, of not having the chocolate crust on the ice cream bar flake off in our mouths like a dark Christ Host. I see in my neighbors' eyes incomprehension first, then disbelief. The boy has misread the headline... He is joking... When I insist that Pearl Harbor has been bombed by the Japanese they rush into the house to turn on the radio. I go home to enlighten my parents.

Pearl Harbor. Hawaii. Japan. How tiny and far away the dots appear on the map. Smaller than Los Angeles where I am surrounded by horizons on all sides. Smaller than my appetite, than my looking forward to supper and all that . Besides, there is that huge stain of blue between Japan and us. Even between Hawaii and the coast of California. I know I am still alive; even if I wanted to carry on as the adults are, I still have my homework to do. And there's the unfinished box of sugar wafers Celia Iglesias gave us just yesterday, wafers for which I have not lost any degree of lust.

Strange that we should have enemies. More unimaginable still that they should come after us or we go after them. But it happens, grindingly. There is a whole science to finding enemies, to aiming guns and draining an otherwise cowardly person of all blood. To do such things one needs hate and that is quickly manufactured. In no time at all Japan is pictured in the media as a nest of depraved yellow monsters. The strait-jacket of ideology falls on the lackadaisical spontaneity of everyday affairs and we can no longer imagine there are Japanese fishmonger wives haggling over the price of a fish tail. Or little kids with foreshortened lives.

Los Angeles goes dark at night. Light is curfewed, leaked out in thin strips of fear by careful windows and otherwise hoarded inside houses. Cars move slowly with only their parking lights on. Mother takes fright and she and Father decide we have to leave, go to Mexico where Uncle Rafael and his family live. My older half-brother Alfredo lives there also. What could be better? Why hadn't we realized that that's where we belonged?

It's a weird notion, almost as weird as the war itself, but hither and yon we prepare to march. Our roomers have to find other quarters for themselves: Cook, a New Yorker who smokes such cigars as will make his presence felt long afterwards in the covered porch where he sleeps; Underwood, a writer for the Hollywood Reporter; the British lady who introduced my sister to the British love for tea. It's good-bye to them.

When all is ready, Cook accompanies us to the Greyhound bus station. The parting is made sadder by the fact that he is being inducted into the Army, a man fearful of spiders. Gentle Cook. We see him wave us off and disappear into a night made more dismal by the blackout.

It is four days and nights to Mexico City. We travel like Gypsies. Twenty years later Alfredo will call us Bedouins. Now it's as if we are fleeing an approaching enemy: Father carries Mother's not so portable sewing machine, Mother carries her purse and several blankets to guard off the cold at night, I carry Father's typewriter, and my sister, who has thrown an incredible tantrum and insisted on taking her cat with her, carries the forbidden creature in a large paper sack with handles to it. The cat has been asked not to meow but, naturally, somewhere in endless Texas she makes herself heard. The bus comes to a stop. One would think we were trying to sneak classified information through the bus lines. The bus driver makes a speech about animals not being allowed on board and demands that we get rid of the cat. My sister starts to cry. The more the driver argues the more she cries. We are all wet with her tears.

"Let's go!" a sailor calls out in desperation. He has one more girlfriend to see and one more night to do it in. "Let the kid have her goddamned cat!"

There is a murmur of approbation throughout the bus for this point of view and the bus driver knows he's licked. With a shrug he turns and goes back to his seat. The bus starts swallowing dark miles again and I realize that I never said goodbye to the lady in back who was so kind to me, the one I brought the war home to, who gave me persimmons, who, with her boarder, took my sister and me one night to the Coliseum to watch a massive circus event with Leo Carrillo on horseback and the whole California hoopla, the one for whom each day is a nation of light, who lives in the shadow of disaster safe because America proves large and because America is large and Pearl Harbor so small. Oh, let me tell you, Pear Harbor is so small. Only the fanaticism of a few military men in Japan could have conceived of so small a plan. Only they could have had so small a thought, a thought that falls below the scale of thought, past zero, into the storerooms of Hell. One knows what they were thinking. It's so simple, so easy. Use force. Conquer. We have the right. Down with the insolent white race.

They forgot that such thoughts harbor daemonic consequences. While thinking these thoughts in their war rooms they might have felt a chill in the air and reached for their coats. What they put on was the mantle of ashes that befell Hiroshima, the blanket of death that covered Nagasaki, as if the chill would never leave the world again. It is a certainty. The Buddha put it very well: everything is thought, everything mind. The earth is waiting for us to realize how long a furrow each thought plows into time, into the horizon where the atom splits into the unity of disaster. It waits for us to learn once and for all how many weeds spring up if we don't tend our gardens.

6
INTERMEZZO

Without innocence how the world is dancing, dying. The world and not the earth. Not the earth yet because it has its valid eucalyptus groves, its meadows, its ignorant oceans and its Nubian goats. We in Mexico, the four of us first thing off feeling more like foreigners than we had in the U.S. The sense of walls in an apartment, in a cul de sac near Buccareli and the Reloj Chino during endlessly hourless 1942. Confusion. Parents not knowing how to make a living and I awash in the city with cousin Sischo, the least magic of Uncle Rafael's four magic, miraculous and strange offspring. Sischo who more than I knows just how close sex is to enthrall us for keeps. Who takes me to somber palaces where a rotund little man is painting miles of frescoes and to museums where double-headed creatures sleep the disturbing sleep of formaldehyde. Who leads me to woebegone villages mortgaged in mist whence we climb mountains thinly pined, salted with snow, hungry, coming back at dusk gangly and life-denied as boys are.

Dislocated from Los Angeles, self-exiled from Costa Rica, driven to the flower of muck that is Mexico, this quartet a disconsolate disconsulated Father of stitches, a Mother of warmth, a daughter of meows and a son of letters. Swindle us out of nothing, Mexican crooks. Laugh at Mother in the street for wearing pants when with the years every tamale-shaped Mexican woman will waddle down the boulevards with her ass in a near-splitting nylon obscenity. And half-brother Alfredo contributing to the chaos, coming home now that he

lives with us, drunk, injured, but somehow writing the loveli-
ness of things like

poetry
the world that you are
trembles on the jubilant
forehead of air

with a pen dipped in gum arabic to hold and in guardian angel
blood to keep and in future Zapotec virginities to prosper.

But, wait! They are calling you, nervous boy! To the grave! To
the catacombs! To the bite of bat tooth and the suck of
vampire thirst! To lie frozen with terror every night in bed
after reading Sischo's dark comic books in which ghouls wander
the sunless streets in search of victims. Nightmare world that
becomes mine as I hold the books with sweaty hands unable to
stop reading, looking fascinated with the hopelessness of the
self caught in its fear of death, a death without transfiguration
except into evil chasms as if man's evil had transcendental
properties when it doesn't. It doesn't.

But the night comes relegating me to my room with its blank
walls and its one ominous window. There I tremble. In bed I
sweat a cold unfiltered essence of fright, unable to move, eyes
fixed ahead waiting for the arrival of the ectoplasmic goo that
with icy fingers will probe the foot of the bed, move up and
find me, find my soul, devour it above my dismembered body.

Delivered to a pitiful weakness, a destiny of shadows that claim
more than their parental objects were willing to grant them
inching out and taking over, nibbling at the light at the edges
of my nervous system. I don't tell Sischo, don't tell my parents.
Everything is okay, I say to them when they don't ask. In the

daytime, oh small respite, everything seems normal, nobody notices I am turning paler, growing thinner, bags beneath my eyes. Then with evening again the imagination runs away from itself. In the streets the tortilla makers bend over their charcoal fires gaining strength from the odor and the warmth, but I have no such source of security, no pocket of flame to keep away the shades of Hell. In other bedrooms my sister sleeps soundly, my parents sleep soundly, and the niggardly noises of the night mean nothing to them, they don't hear them. The plumbing gurgles indecently, a cat yowls some-where on a roof, a window jars open or closed, a car horn hounds a drunk off the pavement. I lie alone to hear these pregnant sounds deliver sinister children. They multiply and gather around me. The way they have wormed themselves out of pure silence suggest unspeakable danger.

Sleep comes later. After an agony of waiting for that hand to touch the foot of the bed. Then it's morning. The victory of the morning is only temporary, a reprieve of a few hours before the sun goes down and I am a day weaker. A day closer to the encounter. The habit of fear has made inroads. My hands tremble, I have lost all appetite, I am a secret horror comic book junkie.

And then, as if it had been a dream, the fumes evaporate. What frees me is the decision to return to Los Angeles. We can't continue to live on borrowed time, no means of livelihood. In a barbaric and alien city that wants no *pochos*, as Latins who live or come from the States are called. The Japanese seem stalemated across the immense checkerboard of the Pacific and once again the California of my mother's family's dream begins to tug. The Bedouins move again with less money now so it's into a dull three story brick apartment building just west of Downtown.

Mother gets employment right away and my sister and I are packed off to school. Belmont High for me where nothing is taught. Where a couple of gym coaches scrutinize my neck claiming in my presence that the vertebrae above my shoulders that stick out are a sure sign I am Jewish.

The neighborhood is nearly New Yorker in appearance. Somber. No-nonsense buildings, none of the pretty stuff, no gardens. Across the street a garage where cars have come to be disenchanted with speed. The dour repairman owner is never far from the entrance. Expecting the arrival of a job challenging enough to put him to work. Next to him there is a storefront grocery where milk has recently gone from ten to eleven cents a quart. In a cement area in back of the apartments utterly devoid of charm the trash bins are always full with the lampsidivies Americans love to throw away. Orphanannies my sister and I try to convince Mother to adopt. Without success.

Characteristic of this period, perhaps because my sister and I had no friends at all and had to fall back on each other, is how much we fought, We fought with words and with our hands, scratching and hitting each other. She was every bit my equal in both departments. We would fight and then the storm would pass. Whatever anger we felt didn't leave any permanent marks and after this period we accepted one another, found our separate things to do and got along fine.

With her light complexion and brown hair, she took after the Cardona side of the family while I, with my curly hair and darker skin, was more like the Hines.

Being three years apart in age we never went to the same schools and never shared the same concerns. While I began to gravitate towards science she took up the violin and scratched away at at with some consistency if no particular aptitude. But it was as if a field had been planted which would bear fruit some thirty years later, when her daughter Dylana would win the silver medal at the Tchaikovsky Competition in the Soviet Union, playing on a borrowed violin worth hundreds of thousands.

Around the block, in a wooden house too nondescript to describe, live acquaintances from Costa Rica. A mother, a father, a son about 18 who suffers from epilepsy and needs a partner to go peeping tomming after supper. I like him. I go. With a weasel's instinct for nests he finds the windows behind which women dress and undress.

The building at the corner. I tell him it's too exposed but he fears nothing. What if the cops drive by, what if the garage man looks our way, he's standing there in front of his shop in the middle of the block smoking a cigarette.

"No. He won't do anything!"

"He's looking at us!"

"So what! People never do anything. I've told you how I go to movie theatres and walk right into the ladies room. Nobody stops me. I go into one of the johns and when a woman enters the one next to mine I peek from underneath. The most I get is a dirty look."

My guilt makes me think the man can read our minds. Max shrugs his shoulders and peeks through a window. He calls me over to look. The blind has been left an inch or two above the closing point. I peek and see furniture, a living room.

Hear the voices of two women, one close. I draw back. Max holds me by the scruff of the neck. And suddenly. From a door. Naked. Holding a towel. A naked woman, my first, my only, gorgeous, round, in a blinding second. Red hair in the crotch, the holiest. I pull away electrified and when Max pulls me back she's no longer there. She's no longer there for years in a row. But it's enough if I disregard the lust for more. Enough. A vision, a treasure stolen there in wartime L.A. for me to blunderingly grow by.

I never see her again, I don't go with Max any more. It's enough. Too scary. I have seen it and I can wait, wondering why it is so utterly forbidden, why nakedness is so distant from the animal wanting, from the wish to pay homage, from the dream of the someday electrical contact. I carry her everywhere with me, to school, mouthing a harmonica I will never master. To used bookstores Downtown. To bed, to the bathroom. Until she diminishes in size, grows vague, ambiguous, faint, and shreds. Until my imagination cannot conjure her and she's no more, no more. Except as myth. As myth she continues and she grows. She prospers. There is nothing anybody can do to take her away from me, she doesn't age, she doesn't move, she has just taken a shower, she comes in to chat, oblivious, drying her head. It is an instant, a crucial moment, what I will call fifty years later radical. A radical moment. When you are totally awake, frightened, shocked, in possession. You possess her because she's more real than breakfast, than light. She's everything you want, have wanted, will want. She's want itself boiled down to the reason why we come alive, why we crawl on this planet and exult. Beyond her triangle of stiff hair is dreamed softness, tunnelings, echoes, laughter, new life. Not consciously so. Patently. Breathlessly. Undeniably. To imagine that those two legs could open, that the bush could yield to reveal the seashell, the roar of the sea, the majesty, is to begin.

The stench of death remained behind, in Mexico. Back in the U.S. I am fearless and committed. Committed and resolved and ready and willing and patient and breathless. In one word, I am in torment. But deliciously so. In my body, bells are waking everybody. My heart hears them and begins pumping not only blood but want. My brain hears them and starts to glorify the words of alertness and the voices of angels. Hallelluia! I am safe in a dark time. I am lost and insignificant but my every move is toward synthesis, the union of my flesh with others. No tree of justice, no song of splendor will ever flower without the driving will to crash into that camp so close and yet so distant, so everlastingly far away from Yeats, the Irishman's excrement.

7

THE DARK OF THE MOON

The rains won't stop. Everything is sodden and heavy and dark with night. The nights bend together in an arc to crush the importance of the days. The ferns and succulents at knee level and the berry bushes above them make the path on the side of the apartment narrow with their greenness and wet with rain. This is the path outside the kitchen door, which we use to go to the small garden in back or to the street. We don't use the front door of the house since it opens onto the living room and that has been turned into my bedroom.

The path belongs to the snails. One has to be careful; they make an awful crunching sound when stepped on. In the mornings, these dubious mornings when we rush out to go to school or work, it is hard to remember. My parents disappear through that path like ghosts; they go first. Then my sister and I follow. I am the last to leave the apartment because the back side of Los Angeles High School is across the street from us.

I sleepwalk over. The four of us are really asleep or half awake, caught in our own and half the world's nightmare, in a time of grief. The war is going badly, nobody knows how to carve a carcass and the small change the world had to spend on music is lost in muck. Everything is unreal, silvery in the weak wet light of this cursed year moist with a hundred thousand deaths. Los Angeles is not so much a city as a dampened park where faint events take place. Each person one meets in the fog carries with him or her the diffuse, opaque, unlocalized sound of a buried gun, of an underground explosion no one can afford to hear, let alone claim responsibility for.

It's up to me to lock the kitchen door. Not that there are any thieves left. It is not a time for petty stuff like that and all the criminals are celebrating in the beer halls of Germany. But I lock up anyway. Immediately as I turn to do so the bushes soak me with the water they spared my parents and my sister. To four disparate points in the city we take this moisture, and the sun never shines enough to dry us. Everything vital seems so far away. We are newly alone in the country, isolated from everyone, made to feel our sobriety in the taste of our nearly empty glasses, fearful of every step.

Mother takes the Olympic bus a block away and goes downtown to work in the garment industry. Intemperate sewing machines swallow her fingers, all of the energy there, leaving them so dry the rest of her life she'll pluck at her hangnails no matter what she's doing until she draws blood. She has never been so nearly out of dreams as she is now. And Father, without an ounce of English, labors somewhere in Hollywood gluing plastic soles onto cheap shoes. He comes home smelling of disgraced concordance, of insults, of a brew made from the bones of horses. He can't get the hang of it. The job requires the skill of a man used to using his hands and Father has never had to work with them. All he can do is type sixty words a minute with two fingers. His foreman is constantly urging him to go faster with the gluing and when Father can't get the soles to sit right on the shoes on a first twist of the wrist, the man flares up, hurls the mishandled shoe at the wall and ridicules him.

Father seems to have lost that thin veneer of self confidence he had gained—not through the mediocre jobs his timidity had always found him in Costa Rica—but through the inner world he had forged out of much reading, out of his passion for the transcendent and the little bit of writing he had done for the lost cause of Central American unity. So here is this hunter, not of raw meat, but of ideas, reduced to impotence by a bully with a toothpick in his mouth yelling obscenities at him.

At home, wearing an apron, he cooks for us. Mother comes home the last, exhausted, and if we had to wait for her to cook we wouldn't eat till nine. The meals are those of a rookie cook and we eat glumly, without a single stitch of laughter.

Finding themselves off center, fearing that they have made a profound mistake in coming to a brutal country, Mother and Father quarrel incessantly. My sister and I soften the silence between the words they will be sorry for later with the silence of prospective orphans. The intensity of the anger is frightening and new. We don't know what to say or do except when our parents threaten to go their separate ways. Then we cry and plead with them not to do such a thing. We feel abandoned already; in our hearts there is the horror of perhaps not seeing one or the other of them ever again, of being placed in a foster home.

When the fighting is over, the ensuing peace is threatened by the next storm, coming, we know from experience, right on the heels of the preceding one. We prepare for it by having omens for breakfast, nightmares for dreams, discreet disasters in place of everyday events. One day the fight is because the omelet we are served can't be cut: It is full of hairs. Obviously it has been dropped on the floor but Father won't admit it. Another time my sister nearly passes out for lack of oxygen in the closet where she likes to go sit and do her dreaming. Yet we go on, day after day, forgetting who we are, eating in memory's name, the four of us shaken, knowing that for many reasons we can't ever return to Costa Rica. Dreams cannot be knifed like that. Costa Rica, the little diamond we knew at cradle time, has sunk to the bottom of the sea. It has ceased to exist.

Saplings do not return to their nursery. My favorite book is a history of biology; I am busy identifying with the men who first explored that continent, looking at everything I can think of with my microscope, the medley of organisms in green water, running around, duplicating and gobbling each other up, my illicit semen trying to wiggle out of the microscope's compound gaze. Miss Kennedy, my biology teacher, encourages me to think that there is a future somewhere under the rubble of the universe. With hair pulled back in puritanical fashion, she encourages us to dissect and draw grasshoppers and frogs as if they didn't stink of formaldehyde. For everything I do she gives me an A. I want to reciprocate, lead a life of devotion, die for science, give my parents a window to look out of.

But I have no such intelligence. I am stuck, even this early and without knowing a thing about it, in the static ways of the visionary. My nature is to see one thing and have it reverberate outward in concentric light rays. It either fades into space, making concerted study impossible, or the rays, after spreading uselessly for decades, alight on a definition for my life such as Blake's *energy is eternal delight*. When this happens then doors into the creative open for me. Epiphanies can occur any time, through odors or passageways such as the place outside the kitchen, glistening in the rain.

Right now it has chosen to rain over Los Angeles as never before, as never afterwards. It's as if the skies had to weep for so deep a war. When the sun shines, the hopeless sunlight comes down as if it were rain, through the vapors that it generates on the asphalt and the warped roofs. On Olympic, a great dane runs in front of a bus; I document the weld of toenails and screeching brakes, the single thump of death. Then, in the silence after the bus and everyone has gone, the body by the gutter. I stare uncomprehendingly as it begins to rain again. I head to a wider home past a narrower entrance path and I smell the Jewish neighbors' cooking.

Time and again the four of us do nothing but get past days that have no vertebrae. I spend my late afternoons in the library which faces the school. This is two blocks away, across Olympic. I love its brick housing, the garden it sits in, the lavender flowers on the trees leading up to it. Those trees have leaves of a brownish green, shaped like those of chirimoya trees. In my fantasies, I am transported back to the highlands of my country while I sit in elegant surroundings where everything is reverent silence and absorption. The oak chairs and solid oak tables, the hushed religiosity of the place, all lead to contemplation and day dreaming. I like reading though I retain nothing. I like looking at the mug shots of gangster bacilli. They speak to me, I hear them talking among themselves with tiny voices. They are all faintly sexual in appearance, little hairy sausages or rods that secrete the chemicals of death unless they are bred in captivity, as Pasteur did with *Bacillus anthracis*. This was the great breakthrough in bacteriology in the 19th century. Pasteur cultivated the bacillus in chicken broth and found that after a few generations, the little guys had lost their weapons. Their virulence could not kill a mouse. It took a stroke of genius to conceive the next step: He inoculated animals with the cultivated bacillus and then, when he reinoculated them with the anthrax bacillus in its wild form he found that he had rendered the beasts immune.

These accounts are as exciting as the tales of Homer or Jules Verne; they come dressed in a language full of multisyllabic words, with heroes named Metchnikoff, van Tieghem and Leeuwenhoek. With the afternoon rain washing the leaded windows of the library clean I sit and mouth the words. Schizomycete, Microspira comma, scheroidal colony, plasmolysis, arthosphore, zoogloeae....

I take the books home, I smell them for their subtle paper and glue odors, I caress them and browse through them. I am dreaming science without accumulating knowledge. I invent projects that get me good grades but mean nothing. They satisfy a curiosity that will eventually transform my microscope into a piano and let my hunger slide for fifty years into the untenable future. I place newborn fish in wads of wet cotton and look at the circulation of the blood in their tails. I draw the webs of capillaries going every which way like one-lane country roads, filled to capacity with platelets bumping along like Model A's. Then I put the tiny fish back in the aquarium before the master switch of their hearts goes out and the roads are clogged with lifeless wheels.

There is a sense of awe in all this but it's private and intermittent. The rest is loneliness, a school of life without friends, moss growing from cracks in the cement path at home, the merchant ship of the moon in drydock over San Pedro. Our souls have turned into bitter raincoats. Each night four black umbrellas bathe in the darkness like silken hippopotamuses, like the unimposing four ravens of a lesser apocalypse. I hear them skittering across the floor, their now dry wings flapping in aborted flight. Cold sweat collects on their witch-like faces and I am ill in the endless night, with dawn for vomit.

The consolations are few but it's only fair to name them. There is Miss Kennedy. She keeps pointing in one direction, setting me on course, but then she retires, at the end of the school year. I go into her classroom at the end of the last bell, to say goodbye, and she gives me her staple remover as a gift, letting me glimpse another immensity, a lonely life, this one already knee deep in its estuary.

There are the neighbors. We are too indrawn to engage them as a family but I've made the acquaintance of the two teenagers, older than I, a boy and a girl who share my sympathy for Russia, for that misunderstood, exotic experiment only the Slavic soul could even think to undertake. To that extent the war becomes dream, possibility. We are, some of us, a life away from knowing redemption cannot be gained through force, but I am here speaking of small consolations during the dark of the moon, of the tunnels that make communication possible at all, the underground sewers that imitate the plumbing of our bodies, where we live, where the Jews of Poland hide, and it's a way of life next door to death and promise. Innocent then, unaware of the Gulags, we think we have found answers. In this way each generation is manipulated forward by some false Messianic force. We are no different. To us, the Russians are a splendid people fighting with all they have, their wounded blood in the freezing wind.

The kitchen path is overgrown. The hedge grows small berries I have learned to like for their lemony flavor. The books I don't really read give me the sense that life is on-going, that it might start up anytime soon. In the meantime, with my clothes slightly moist, my understanding is that I belong here, by the kitchen door, trying to reach a berry, not quite one with the life of others, of my family or the neighbors on the other side of the hedge. What I hear are a few inaudible voices that provide comfort, especially the voice of the teenage girl. The timbre of her voice is produced in a throat whose particular acoustics duplicate her warmth. She will always have that; she will go through life choosing circumstances that match that almond flavor. And so, as I reach for a berry high enough to be wanted, I select Eleanor's melody to guide my hand and I am comforted. The epiphany, indestructible and brief, makes for center sun in a time of annihilation, as if a ship dismantled by a storm were being reassembled in the amber fathoms of a caressing voice, bound for a kingdom of modesty and ever-ranging goodness.

I begin to cry standing still. Or is it the rain on my face beginning its sonata for the men being torn to bits in the snowy reaches of their Novgorov land, for my parents somehow lost in the same battle? Somebody is weeping, making sounds in the throat of the bell of churches just as my sister is playing with the toys that are her future children. All future happenings are echoes of my standing here, a kid having his lesson in timelessness, stuck in the honey jar of illusion, his hand a mudra of desire.

Mother and Father are starting to make up. My sister and I pretend that their fight last night is of no consequence. They are in the kitchen having breakfast with silent words of affection. It is Sunday and the sun is a heavy silver coin pushed fast by bands of clouds. A clothesline full of sparrows chatters away in the backyard. I will stand here until I don't have to amount to much. My ambitions will be inconsistent.

Ghost pieces of me will deliver their solid moments at the appropriate times and no one will be the wiser. The book I am holding in my other hand falls to the ground, awakening me, spilling bacilli from its pandora box of leaves. The sparrows scatter. In each sparrow beak we are carried elsewhere. And we go willy nilly.

8
THE RENEWED BRIGHTNESS

The stars of fortune change for us when Mother decides to buy the house on 6210 Fountain Avenue. It is a daring leap, from being anonymous and woebegone to having a place we can call our own, with a hibiscus bush in front, daisies in back paralleling the driveway all the way to the garage, trees and a climbing rose bush knocking on the back door with pink knuckles. The front has a low brick wall protecting the entrance way, which is large and shaded, a perfect place to sit and read a book when it is too warm to stay indoors.

How Mother has accomplished this is a mystery I can't fathom. And she doesn't like to speak of such things because it would undermine the strict economic discipline by which we live. But it's obvious that she's managed to hang on to some of the money that got us here from Costa Rica, and that her take-home pay from the garment factories hasn't all been spent on the daily grind. She's fabulous that way although it makes for those light meals and skimpy Christmases my sister and I have learned to take for granted and for which Father has the appropriate Spanish proverb, delivered with a twinkle in his eye. "La necesidad tiene cara de caballo." he'll say. "Necessity has the face of a horse." And one pictures the terseness and resignation on the face of a work horse in a stony field somewhere in Spain.

Each of us has gained a new lease on life; the sun has begun shining again, the war begun to be won. For me, personally, contentment lies in the fact that I have been allowed to remain at L.A. High where I am on speaking terms with three or four students and where I like a few teachers. Three, to be exact: The aposiopetic chemistry teacher who, when he stops in mid-sentence, gets lost looking out the window with his dreamy blue eyes, the English teacher who mesmerizes the entire class each time she pulls a handkerchief out of her desk and blows her nose in an elegantly elephantine manner and, of course, the ghost of Miss Kennedy, whose faint odor of virginity clings to the hallway by what used to be her room.

By rights, living in Hollywood now, I should be going to Hollywood High but I didn't want to be in a new school, my fourth in three years, and the authorities concurred. It means I have to transfer buses to get there but that is nothing to me. The first bus goes down Vine Street, which becomes elegant Rossmore. Where Rossmore ends, on Wilshire, the bus turns, goes down a ways then finds and follows Crenshaw. I transfer on Crenshaw and Olympic. A year from now this route is going to turn into bliss but I don't know this yet; for the present, I am content to speed past the houses of the rich, knowing that they belong to those who look at them with wonder.

I try to solve the mystery of the rich. Do they exist? As the bus passes one magnificent mansion after another I wonder why I never see a single soul coming in or out of them; why their stately gardens are frozen in a state of perfection. The tall sycamores over the English style houses have learned not to shed a single leaf, the royal palms curving with the driveway of a Spanish villa are each a clone of one another.

Though we live a block from the Ranch Market, our neighborhood is relatively quiet and clean-cut. It is certainly much more human. It is one of those neighborhoods which only thirty years from now will begin to look disheveled enough to bring on the inevitable apartment complexes. Things happen in it. Kids play games on the sidewalks, mothers hang clothes on clothes lines, occasionally and absent-mindedly pinning down a cloud instead of a sheet. A discreet kind of chaos is part of the equation. Our street is bordered on both sides by trees of a dense, disorganized kind of foliage which insists on shedding narrow, brownish leaves the whole year long but which provide shade and perhaps dampen some of the city noise. These trees are strictly anonymous. I have asked neighbors, the mailman, and the grackles who live in them, but no one seems to know what they are called. Grackles build their nests in the formidable interiors, careless about nomenclature; their family quarrels go on all day and when they are not busy screeching, they prey on pedestrians, diving at their heads with the intention of tearing off some hair to use on their nests. Whoever will some day write the filmscript for Hitchcock's "The Birds" must live on a street with similar aviatory conditions.

Our two neighbors are, on one side, Mrs. Jorganson, a potentially irascible German widow who is nice to my sister and, on the other, an old couple slowly sinking into oblivion. One never sees them, never hears these folks. At the corner, a retired dentist still plies his trade if you go knock on his door.

Everything is conveniently close: cleaners, barber, hardware store, movie house. On Vine, half a block away, across from the Ranch Market, a blue Van de Kamps bakery in the shape of a Dutch windmill supplies Mother and me with our tea-time pastries: pecan coffee cakes and pineapple bear claws. I say Mother and me because Father doesn't have a sweet tooth and my sister is too young to realize the importance of tea-time. Kittycorner from the Ranch Market is a lone hotdog stand unaware that in a few years it must give way to a huge radio station complex. From there, looking north, one can spot the Miller's Highlife beer sign atop one of the tall buildings on Hollywood and Vine. At night the sign bubbles with neon colors: a female harlequin wearing a short, flared skirt and a pointed hat sits perilously close to the edge of the abyss toasting a new moon with an elegant glass of beer as it fills up with liquid gold.

And I am home, becoming more intimately myself. All of us are living with renewed brightness, or with problems lit up from within. That is the thing about brightness. It isn't only the product of the sun but what the sun can engender in the darkness of time and in the wishes of the human heart. Father is in the garden every day, making it sing. Mother sews at home now, working for some lady on Hollywood Boulevard. My sister has been granted a dog. We'd ask life to stop if it could; that is, to go on being good for us. But, of course, even now, we are made of string balls and unwinding roads, of eventual separation.

The brightness notwithstanding, coming of age is lightning slow. And deafeningly silent. For me, the first few changes have to do with a more acute sense of my own spaces and with the first explorations of sound. I sleep in the covered porch to the side of the house, which in winter is the coldest room, and the hottest in summer. I don't mind. Having a room of my own for the first time is exhilarating. It's like having frontiers and privacy, like having moments to oneself and places to be without having to be anywhere. The walls are mine and I can put things on them that shout back my name. The ceiling is mine to contemplate when I lie down on my bed. And I have a desk and a chair and a dresser. It's hard to know what to do with all the light that floods in, and with the babble from the little radio I've put together from bits and pieces. In the evenings I use earphones, that way I can listen and do my homework as late as I want to without disturbing anyone in the house.

With the radio I encounter a grid of sound for which I have no map. The patterns are contradictory. What I hear is sometimes beguiling, other times bombastic and empty. Even the sublime has to be learned, how much more so the mundane. First, it is all remarkably the same; it is only with patience that one begins to discern the differences. With music I am getting involved in the first transactions of distance. It's the luminosity of the room I have inherited at last. As if chance had placed my soul in the shipyard at the end of the world, where the greater ribcage of a sailing vessel is being built, with materials assembled at random. I don't even know jazz from tin pan alley, pop from classical. I listen without qualification while a history, a landscape, forms around me. This is the inner neighborhood, as full of static as the outer one, but one full of endless journeys into formal silence.

The problem is that I spend too much time in it. It makes me unpredictable.

The family is put off by my moodiness, unaware that, like a miner who has stumbled upon a mother lode, I want to shout and keep my secret at the same time. They want conformity, meals taken at prescribed times, school attended daily. School, where work in subjects grotesquely off the mark must be completed and graded in just six ways, the A to F's of mediocrity, with no end in sight.

My trouble, my itch, the sudden revelations, the revolts, occur outside the surety that was childhood. Any new footing is deceptive, momentary. What it is is that the brightness of our new life has coincided with the very different brightness of my growth, they are unbalanced and rich enough to form a vivid darkness. Darkness is not just in the rain, in fallen petals, it is in being illiterate and misunderstood in worlds tightly packed one against the other.

Restless, I spill out of the house. Into a town of poinsettias tall as giraffes, a city of small shops with dusty windows. In one of these I buy a Bible which I will never read; in another a wooden flute which I never learn to play. In second hand bookstores I paw through books I will not return to for years, not until their authors can bring me to life with their paper eyes years, eons later. Some afternoons, longer than others, I attend free radio shows. Harry James plays his facile trumpet up near Hollywood and Vine, on a bright stage a million miles from where I sit darkly in the mainly empty theater, he making money out of slick jazz and I wondering why I know nothing at all.

Mine is a seemingly empty sixteen-year-old life absolutely devoid of meaning and hence miraculous: an experiment in the neutral agar of isolation. I live suspended in time, buffeted by tides of sunlight, by days reflected on glass. In our back-yard I look at the flowers and they mirror the madness of sexual need. They are virulent in color, capricious in shape, odorif-erously moist, petulant in their young beauty, rank in decay. The insects that attend them are rapt slaves; theirs is the single-mindedness of a season's survival. They zigzag rapidly through a neighborhood of sudden death burning their gas tanks furiously so that their progeny can do the same thing, when they hatch under the hennish sun in a year they'll never see.

But the strangest thing of all occurs when this unkempt garden of the world impinges directly as essence, as promissory note to the ecstasy I know should be mine. More than once I am drawn to a low, ramshackle building on Fountain and Highland, a couple of miles from home. It's a second-hand shop selling more dust than gadgets but the gadgets are nearly as infinite. All of the parts of machines and appliances that have ever fallen off the main component are represented here incognito. And all the pans, pots, tools, furniture, harnesses, faded reproductions, plaster figurines, lamps, irons, stoves, silverware, crockery and mirrors going back on their promises. The aisles are narrow, the place not so much dark as crowded with tired iridescence. The floorboards yield with each step and the proprietor couldn't care less if one stays there all day. The first time I walked in I experienced a shock. I saw all the things surrounding me with absolute love. I recognized them, not for what they were but for what they were being. I felt welcomed, I felt at home. And it was all clear and significant but so quick. I barely had time to register it before it registered as a doubt. Yet, as aftermath, a good feeling persisted in my chest. Something extraordinary had happened, as if a universe of empty space had manifested itself as a star, glowing and self-assured.

Thankful, I go back often, if only to remember where and how happiness could take place. Especially when habit tends to hand me back my emptiness.

And what does one do with this fantastic grind of inner and outer neighborhoods? The brightness is driving me crazy. And the world is the flower. I am just a bug; I wander the length of Hollywood Boulevard looking into shops, handling objects that arouse my curiosity until they fade in a sudden squall of boredom. I walk far down Sunset Boulevard, far up Santa Monica Boulevard searching for the angels I can't see. I comb the neighborhood looking at the houses for answers to my undefined enigma. Is it only a hormonal imbalance that has stolen that delicious fraction of a second assurance I felt at the second-hand shop? I know that behind windows and doors other lives are taking place, and I want to know what they mean, and if they have a perfume. Do they undress to glorious bodies that live forever? Do they sing silently in ecstasy at having arrived at a place where things make sense? I don't know and I want to know. I look at passersby, examining them for signs of that knowledge I am sure exists but hasn't been explained to me, hasn't revealed itself in a wolf's fang (where would I come across such a thing!) or a raven's shadow (where indeed!). Knowledge I can't name, wisdom I can't talk about. So much so that with those closest to me I have to pretend the hardest I am not in pursuit of such ephemeral issues. Father, for instance, could never be approached with it. He is the furthest away, the most unreachable, because of that proximity which is the repudiated, the cast-off past that produces the questions.

What I do is wait and watch. Rodolfo comes from Costa Rica, Rodolfo our cousin, tall, lanky, about twenty. And I watch him. We sleep on bunk beds in my porch and I watch him read a great thick tome on Johann Sebastian Bach. He enrolls at the university almost the same day he arrives in a taxi after having slept in a seedy hotel in downtown L.A. and he's studying this man named Bach. Who exactly is this man named Bach? What neighborhood does he fit in, what sublimation of brightness can he apport and how is he related to this thin cousin of ours who talks to me about an 18th century Germany full of organists, who works in a camera shop part time and is gentle as silk? I am in the school of chaos and Rodolfo is at a coolly formulated stage of development I can't touch, where everything connects and is manly, elegant and directional.

At L.A. High, using a handle I have on reality, I argue politics with a few boys during our lunch hour, sitting in an empty classroom with our Spanish teacher (I am enrolled in her class so as to learn English grammar by indirection). She sits and lets us talk, seldom participating because she is temperamentally too sweet to see the use of ripping things apart with ideas. I like to shock her with my adherence to utopian Communism but she sees through me. In her house, where she lives with her old parents in a space squeezed together by hills, she walks the elongated hallways with a porcelain bowl of green grapes in her hand, almost smiling because she's thinking of me, because she knows I will never endanger America with my muddled dreams but save her from the sterile condition of being single and unattractive by practicing with her, she with her slightly imperfect Spanish, this language of impossible dreams, this tongue of early dawn that makes her life improbably possible.

As I say, I know nothing. But with her the few times she has given me a ride home in her car, as with the junk at the second-hand shop, I have felt the nearness of a connection that is all that counts. By the immediacy of the cosmos I am everything. I am touched and brought to life by the oxygen of our opaque existence, by this contract to exist jointly in time and space, in a double-jointed neighborhood, a paradox.

9
PORTRAIT AT TEATIME

Mr. Footernak drops in a teatime. He doesn't drink tea but prefers to sit a little distance away smoking his cigar and sharing with Mother and me this feeling (that tea brings) that the afternoon is the perfect time for the fellowship of small talk. Small talk masks, of course, depths we tacitly recognize in need of masking. Perhaps only for lack of training (philosophical) but also because we know small talk to be the perfect vehicle to arrive at any depth without becoming self-conscious about it.

It is small talk, after all, that slowly reveals each to the others. Each of us is so different that anything more direct and intentional would wreck the delicious harmonies of the hour. Mr. Footernak, as the now countless afternoons have revealed, is a Jewish gentleman of undisclosed means (he hasn't gotten to that yet), retired from the garment trade and living in Hollywood in a sort of limbo made possible by the overly kind weather, the palm trees, and the fact that his health still allows him to smoke.

Compare him to Mother or me and you will see that what takes place so often around three in the afternoon at 6210 Fountain Avenue (five scant blocks from Hollywood and Vine) should be considered a kind of minor miracle. Mother, a woman of sixty (is it sixty? No. I am wrong. It's forty-nine! Amazing), pleasant, intelligent, imported (from Costa Rica), doing piece work at home for Miss Kelly (hence Footernak), the proprietor of a brassiere store on Hollywood Boulevard. Perhaps what is most attractive about my mother is her middle-class background, proper, cautious, educated and sensible.

I am a smallish, shy boy of seventeen in the eleventh grade, bouncing between a former choice of science and a growing but impossible-to-manage passion for composing music) and currently reading *Jean Christophe* at a fast clip.

It is 1943 and neither Mr. Footernak nor we know anything about Nazi atrocities against Jews. We comment on the progress of the war as unassuming bystanders and have no inkling that the new and final age of man is about to be ushered in in about two years when Hiroshima (a city we have never heard of) is turned into dust and ashes by the propositions of Albert Einstein. Jesus. No. We vegetate at the ecstatically ignorant level of the underbrush if this world is a jungle. Through no fault of our own since history is never shared or understood beforehand, obviously, or on a current basis. Only later, when it is too late and one, older then, also realizes that having understood some horrid little chunk doesn't mean one grasps current horrors.

We three specimens of wartime naivete and existential bliss find pleasure in ourselves, in being little tarnished mirrors to each other at that hour when the human body is balanced between the gorgeous expenditure of morning energy and the descent into evening. A time for tea, or for a cigar, which I have begun to enjoy thanks to Mr. Footernak and the largesse of my mother who only balked initially, fearful that it would impede my growth (my growth being a thing both my parents devoutly and patiently wait for with unlimited apprehension) and which eventually comes in spite of the cigars.

Ah, what don't we talk about! We talk about everything and anything. Knowing it is nothing. So much so I can't recall a single conversation of ours...But why be disappointed? I am in the process of indicating that these conversations serve a different purpose than even we imagine. Conversation, small talk, always has, at all times and in all conditions. It is through small talk, accompanied by related, ubiquitous human gestures, that each of us learns something like the truth about the others.

About Mr. Footernak I have learned so much and in such subtle ways that I must admit language has absolutely no means to convey it. On the other hand, his ways, mannerisms and existence are as real to me at a neural level thanks to small talk as they are impossible to transcribe. What will be missing will be essential and miraculous just as the little I can describe will be essential and miraculous.

About my mother, I can say ever so much more and so much less. To begin with, and aside from her ambition to see the family succeed economically, an ambition that of course consumes most of her waking hours, she is an immense memory bank triggered by pride and contentment. To be of the Hine Pintos from Costa Rica is tantamount to being right, to being tacitly chosen and in proper relation to the Godhead. Not in a pompous or exclusive manner, but through the contentment and the gestures, to go back to that. The body manifests its age and condition aided by a mind that understands its station. In life. In nature. In the order of things. Thus capacity. Mother's capacity stems tacitly from tacitly accepted forces, strengths, family status. The fact that America has reduced her to the level of a glorified garment worker doesn't even touch the elegance, the style, of this being who finds herself privileged to be in Los Angeles placing three meals on the table each day. A privilege and a joy. Hence the contentment, the clear pleasure to be talking with her son and Mr. Footernak about the kind of glue used in the manufacture of shoes or about Chicago's Gold Coast and the kind of winds that blow there.

As her son, I am there as apprentice. I don't know what to but an instinct tells me talking to adults will get me past my overwhelming (and undefined, unrecognized) nihilism, this like mystical desire to convey the odor of geraniums in music, the despair at having seen a particular bunch of weeds at the far end of a backyard once. My impatience with formal learning, a kind of unfortunate disability or perhaps simply the inability to see how harmonic rules relate to dream sound, has led to my abandoning my studies. I am at a standstill, in shock after encountering the stubborn shape of the world, and clinging to these two people in the afternoon (an hour of ease) and knowing that they might at any moment reveal the discolored, the disguised, the magical key to things. Because they are centered in a way that I am not.

Mr. Footernak's way of walking, of entering the house, slowly, ceremoniously, is a key, or part of it. It is ever so much more applicable than a rule of harmony drawn from a Beethoven sonata and made to stand on its own in a bleak textbook. What, to be duplicated? Mr. Footernak walks the way he walks because he is dressed the way he is dressed, in a dark business suit, wearing a tie and sporting cuff links on his shirtsleeves. If somebody had ordered him to wear gym shorts and come visiting he would walk the same way but pain would be visible through it.

He is short and portly and rather funny looking, like one of the more outlandish owls in a bird book. He can hold his humor as it is said some men hold their liquor. Good small talk bordering on gossip brings out a semi-smile on his face and Mother and I try our best to see that that facial expression stays put because it seems to hand back dividends, making us feel terrific. Perhaps because it isn't easy to put it there. Friendship, after all, consists of that, of trying to bring out the signs in a friend that prove one is providing real nourishment, essential nourishment. Mr. Footernak is our friend because, invariably, we make him feel good and because he makes us feel good. Our worlds are so different that we exist and dangle perennially on this rope bridge we have built between our very different shores. He'll bring a message from Miss Kelly and we immediately have a quarter of an hour to talk about how women have dressed through the ages. I listen. What do I know? I might join that conversation from a Marxist point of view since my mysticism (at seventeen) tells me it is time to change the world. Who knows, with equality we might choose to go naked. But anything I say is looked upon as mere improvisation by these two and treated accordingly. The tea is good and we usually have (Mother and I) some pastry from the Van de Kamps blue windmill store across from the Ranch Market on Vine Street.

When Mr. Footernak walks in he takes off his homburg, that landmark, and hands it to me. He knows I will reverentially place it on the mantelpiece out of reach of the cat. He also knows that I look forward to those few seconds it takes me to walk over to the mantelpiece to place his hat there. He knows how I regard that hat. This, again, is inexplicable, for none of us knows how immense a hat is, what it signifies, how it transforms, how it connects, how it echoes the crests of male birds perhaps. The feel of that hat in my hands is unique; it is made from a material (animal fur) with which I am unfamiliar but which my fingers recognize instantly as heraldic. Just as some crazy random chords discovered on the piano are heraldic. And blessed! Oh, why are some things blessed? I want to know, and each time I carry that homburg to the mantelpiece or from it I feel that I am on the verge of solving the mystery.

Like the mystery of very well shined shoes, old shoes that would seem to want to reject such perfection. Mr. Footernak's shoes are entities that do not recognize dust or mud or even smears; like some countries that refuse to recognize others, it's as simple as that. He likes to cross his legs when he sits, so, naturally, the shoes, one at least, comes into more prominence. To be honored. That is what it is saying. Humble things are to be honored, raised from their position of humility and made to shine. If shoes shine, doesn't the soul? That's something very few people understand. In America most men go about with shoes that cry out for a little care. They wear good clothes but the shoes go unserviced. Anyway. The homburg arrives and all the hieratical writing inside, on the hat band. Writing I am dying to read but do not dare, for that would involve turning the hat over in a grossly conscious fashion, as if it were a common object subject to manipulation. It sits on the mantelpiece waiting for its master to decide when it is time to go, waiting for tea to be drunk and for three-fourths of a Churchill cigar to be smoked. Then it goes atop Mr. Footernak, indicating sobriety, propriety and, above all, respect for all men and all things. Oh yes, sorry if this disturbs. Only man's formal gestures can reflect profound respect. I don't any longer trust easy-going clothes or manners to reveal any great state of ease or grace.

Respect for women also. Mr. Footernak has the bearing of a widower (I am guessing this), of a man who has seen a marriage through. As a matter of fact, I believe he has alluded to children in far-off cities. An air of solitude is combined with a more diffident air of sadness. So, naturally, there must be the death of a dear being or of, at least, a close being. Mr. Footernak comes bearing his past just as I, opening the door to let him in, bear witness to eager emptiness. The past is Mr. Footernak. He has brought it to the present by an act of incredible patience that is the process of his personality. A past so strongly there and yet so reserved, so undisclosed. Why? I wonder, knowing little about sorrows.

My mother, being a lady, is precisely what Mr. Footernak needs to recall his wife. Seeing her he wishes life all over again. No matter how different his wife might have been, there is no doubt that here Mr. Footernak revisits femininity, the wonder of the sound of a woman's voice. He is exquisitely proper, of course, a friend of the family, an exile from perhaps some immemorial happiness who, here, in this home, discovers the comfort of an echo, the alacrity of time. Perhaps acceptance only.

I think acceptance plays a major role. The world is all rejection, the cliché of no one giving a damn. But here, in this pleasant small house with the hibiscus bush by the entrance, these strangers turn into friends. Perhaps only acquaintances, people to pass the time with. But who is fooled? Certainly not air, not air that by being in a room gets shared, willy nilly. Taken into the lungs in turn by each person. And thus, how much more so the soul, that unrivaled oxygen, the soul that inhabits or is consciousness and extends variously beyond the body, liking to roam in friendship and in dreams. I spoke of my mysticism. I just want to meet complexity with imagination, the baffling universe with the only faculty that won't reduce it to logic.

Acceptance. A boy with his mouth full of toast talking about not wanting to make money, a frightening prospect for any mother, but taken in stride. Mr. Footernak is of the unspoken opinion that time will change that. By the way Mother takes a sip of her tea she acknowledges that he is right. They do not need to speak at this point. I am saying something nasty about occupations and they know how right it is for a boy of seventeen to be lost, that something might come of it.

The clock strikes a subordinate chime, for it is three thirty, and Father, who has been mowing Mrs. Jorganson's lawn and who can't join us because he doesn't speak English, comes in and says hello. He and Mr. Footernak shake hands like diplomats, a delight. We hear him presently at his typewriter writing a letter to some newspaper in Costa Rica subliminally conveying the wonder that in America one can (the everlasting intellectual) mow lawns at fifty-eight. Shades of Whitman.

My mother cleverly informs Mr. Footernak of her plans to ask for a raise. It is wartime, Miss Kelly has no other source of labor and it is against the law to pay the wages she is paying, not declaring them into the bargain. Something like that. Mr. Footernak understands that he is the fertile middle ground Mother is planting the seeds in. It makes him feel useful. Miss Kelly is a rather volcanic woman who periodically storms our house with supplies and orders. He knows her from way back, from before the Flood, and how perfect it is that Mother needs them and they need her. Best of all possible worlds although in my present phase (Messianic Marxism) I must view it with suspicion.

The raise comes. Not before federal agents for some reason have come and Mother has lied about her earnings, posing as Miss Kelly's business partner. A dangerous moment made more dangerous by my sister (three years younger than I) who, being present, starts to spill the beans to the agents thinking that Mother is stalling because of language difficulties. Saved by a call from Father in the kitchen, who is making rice and needs to know the time so he can time it twenty minutes. Mother looks at the clock on the mantelpiece (famous for being able to include homburgs), yells the time and, in the same breath, all in Spanish of course, tells my sister to get the hell out.

Another digression. But it bears on this world of Mr. Footernak, of making a living in a strange land, of having no choice but to cheat, hurting no one. Mr. Footernak's influence on Miss Kelly is enormous. It isn't for nothing that he has the bearing of an elder statesman. We often wonder what he sees in us and accept his presence in our lives as a benediction. He dispenses a kind of everyday balm. What he might do in an emergency is calm you and call the perfect doctor, or save you with a bit of arcane knowledge, perhaps something from his pocket, it is that ineffable, and that certain.

His hands are minute, a watchmaker's hands. Well-cared for because anyone with spotless shoes would not permit the shadow of dirt under his fingernails. I observe that he converts the dirty habit of cigar smoking into an art. How? By husbanding the ash so that it collects ever so long on the tip of the cigar, a dangerous and forgotten skill (it is told of the great Clarence Darrow that he once mesmerized a jury during a difficult case by driving a wire through the length of his cigar before his opponent rose to summarize his case before the jury. Darrow proceeded to smoke his cigar in a quietly ostentatious manner. The cigar ash went on growing and getting longer until each one of the jurors sat spellbound, watching, unable to follow the intricacies of the prosecution. Legend has it that Darrow won the case, to everyone's surprise) and by being truly decorous about the wet, chewable part. We never see him with a loose, dangling participle of tobacco. Then, also, the quality of what he smokes is so exquisite that even if Mother wasn't a Latin woman and the niece of a cigar-wielding worthy of old, she would welcome the aroma in our house as a salutary addition to our drab olfactory existence.

Invariably at four, after our clock has chimed the hour in the living room, Mr. Footernak double-checks the figure on his vest watch and announces that it is time to be going. I don't show my dismay, for that would embarrass him. Mother suggests he stay longer but everyone recognizes this as a formality. Father abandons the typewriter to come to say goodbye and everyone accompanies him to the door. I bring him the homburg, which he takes from my hands with a smile, as if saying, 'Someday you may wear one…in fact, I know you will,' and he departs, walking, for he has no car, to the bus stop.

He'll be back in a few days, a week at most. In the meantime, Mother and I have our tea each afternoon in the shadow of our great guest, almost turning in his direction (where he usually sits) to verify something or wait for a reply. The tea tastes good, almost as good as when Mr. Footernak is there, but you can stir it all you want, it isn't the same. And yet, we drink our tea as if Mr. Footernak were there, we speak in a different way during that hour, with more formality, with care. In that way, he is almost there, practically there.

And I wonder, who else does he visit when he's not with us? Does he have a circle of friends that he can avail himself of or does he sit at home (what kind of home or apartment or room?) waiting for the time to be right to return? We don't know where he lives, what he does with his time, how he votes, where he eats or banks or shops. We know nothing and we know everything. That he is benign, amiable, clean, careful, diffident but warm, obscure but familiar, rare, useless, private, sorrowful (by inference), lost, forgotten, present by a concatenation of chance and inertia, middle-aged, effective in small matters, pusillanimous perhaps but quite possibly capable of heroic acts, undistinguished but correct, balding, faintly perfumed, possessing (as I think) an immortal soul, coming and going, obviously not at home when he dies, a man, a mensch, a statistic, a friend, a ghost, a memory, a mark, alas, like myself, a bird, a flight.

10
Myrna

Let me call her by her real name. I was going to invent a pseudonym, thinking that she might not like what I say about her but, for me, the name is everything she is. When I think of her I see a white desert, a wasteland of borax extending beneath the heat of August in all directions, as in Death Valley. Only because she said she comes from Bakersfield, from the furnace of the Mohave Desert, and I assumed that Death Valley, borax and lust are synonymous with the simple, dry horror of her town, the searing energy generated in plain white folk there, skin deep beneath the presentable surface.

I know she is going to laugh when she hears this. "Me?" she'll say, "me? A desert? You have to be kidding, kitten! I'm a woman!" She'll pause for an additional thought and then add, "The only thing parched are my lips....and I know how to get relief!"

And wiggling her hips a little more than she has to as she walks between the shelf of glasses and the counter to take a customer's order at the far end, she'll look back and wink at me. So I mean a desert that way, inviting as death, as tumbling down a ravine of heat and exposure.

I am dazzled. We're all cheap that way. There is something shorn, inexpensive and expendable about her and my lust for her. She makes me play for keeps in secret, like a Humphrey Bogart in his teens. Her waitress' wink tells me she sweats just as I do, that she defecates and lives behind the streak of lipstick as if she had brought the anonymous pattern with her. But me, I almost drop the tray of dirty dishes.

She chooses all this shortly before birth, perhaps, or in junior high. She bought herself dirt cheap and decided to carry on and have fun quick. Her legs went round-about what made her available and who the hell was her mother with that broom to tell her no. She left home and never went back.

The name Myrna fits her nervous energy perfectly. It has already been carved on her future headstone by one too many nightcaps at age twenty, when she's still thin and has large eyes and that sailor-devouring hunger rigged up to her genes with a little help from the magazines she reads on her breaks, sitting crosslegged on the counter stool by the kitchen door; magazines which go no further pictorially than showing couples in endless embraces, kissing each other as if that was the solution, the purpose, the answer, the salvation and the sweet bejesus of the body. Body to be wrung dry with little screams that flatten the window blinds against the weakness of the oncoming breeze.

The Thrifty Drugstore is a block down from Hollywood Boulevard, on Vine Street. It is one of an endless chain of drugstores that mark the belly of tinsel town and cater Velveeta Cheese sandwiches for lunch, suppository specials and Baptist druggists uniformed like Nazi experts. The condoms will be hidden until the 70's; the sanitary napkins come in unmarked brown wrappers. What can you do if you are a hypocrite? Things will change one day and become more honest but then other ills and monstrosities will appear and make these social blemishes seem like beauty marks on the face of America.

World War II is going on where the Cliffs of Dover flinch from the pounding. The Germans have gone dark, the Italians grey. Word is that the Japanese take no prisoners; they like confusing human beings with cockroaches. Everyone's off to war. In Los Angeles even a man like my father can get a job. He is near sixty, knows no English and has no experience. He has been an intellectual all his life but he's hired on the spot the day he applies. He's no good at bussing dishes but we need the money and Thrifty can't find anyone else. In fact, they are so desperate that they hire me part time some time later. Father works days and I come in at five and work till nine.

It's a strange experience. Humbling to wear an apron, to have a boss, to be told things to do. But the money is an adventure; immediately I want to start doing things, smoke a pipe, buy more expensive books than before, eat in the cafeteria at school. The job has extraordinary advantages: I can eat all the dough-nuts I want, have waffles with canned peaches on top and be touched by someone who conspires against my peace of mind just for the hell of it.

I curse her. She will be waitressing in drugstore chains the rest of her life. I want her and will be bussing dishes under her upturned nose until the signatures of hell have rubbed off the bark of the first apple tree. I suspect this, I read it later, when I understand the demonized sexual impulse that turns her into a male in pursuit just as it turns me female in my ignorance.

In the narrow hallway upstairs, where the employee dressing rooms are, she and I cross paths and she stops me; she tells me that she thinks I'm cute and, smiling a smile that cannot hide a few bad teeth, she holds me by the shoulders. But she is kind. She probably wants to be kissed, she wants to kiss me and take it from there, start a little something virginal, but she sees the fear in my eyes, the terror at the nearness of what keeps wanting to remain fantasy for a while longer, and lets me go.

What do I know what she is offering? I don't know the line I will cross if I dare kiss her or hold her or something. Sometimes she seems to be merely playing, enjoying going back to school kid stuff; she teases mercilessly, using an overwhelming superiority of weapons, the fruit of her body, the curvature of her buttocks sensationalized by the clear ridge of her panties against the sheer fabric of her white skirt.

Feverishly, for the few hours I work, I do nothing but concentrate on her various taunted secrecies while, somnambulistically, I bus trays of dirty dishes to the kitchen, dump abandoned plates of spaghetti, half-eaten pies and cold cups of coffee laden with cigarette butts into the trash, stash the cutlery near the washing machine where an old Chinaman sweats his double shift and, gagging at the steamy atmosphere of decaying garbage, push open the swinging door and emerge into her world again with empty tray. I see that she is flirting with a nobody, just to keep in practice, to collect a good tip, and she announces that her sailor boy is picking her up at nine.

At nine, upstairs, half-dressed, she peeks out of the women's dressing room when she hears me go by.

"Hey, honey! C'mere!"

Half of her past half a door and half of heaven stop me in my tracks.

"What?" I say stupidly.

"Come here, silly! Tell me if you like this perfume...I'm trying it on the Navy tonight!"

She reaches out her naked arm and I smell it. The perfume is a mask beneath which everything unimaginable will take place in the hours to come while I lie awake in my bed listening to my earphones and wanting to be the unknown sailor dead later in the water or awash even later in the arms of an Italian-American wife back in Hoboken, when the war has turned cold making babies and Stalin is picking at the scab of victory.

The perfume is the door ajar. I reach out and try to touch the neat breast half held by a bra. She parries me with the skill of a matador, frowning, smacking her lips in mock disapproval, and closes the door. Devil! Leaving me trembling and tumescent under the bare lightbulb of desire.

And she emerges all dolled up, masked for unmasking, and gives me a light kiss on the cheek in forgiveness, unaware of the irreparable damage she has done to the edifice of my small wants, that now vast church she has broken into to light dark candles in, insecure and volatile as a vampire near dawn.

And sleepy the next night she smokes a cigarette over a cup of coffee leaning on the counter with dreamy eyes and makes small talk, beautiful when haggard, and full of smiles. My parents, out for a walk—we live five blocks away—walk past the large windows on the side of the drugstore and peer at us. They tap the glass and give me knowing smiles. Their shy son is now talking to women, he's normal after all. Embarrassed, I scurry away to the kitchen with a half full tray of dishes and I hear her laugh. She will always laugh when she sees me or one of my counterparts, the ever weak male, in disarray before her power. The rill of her laughter will preserve her God knows how many decades until one day when gravity will undermine the succulent upbringing of her flesh.

Then she will go on laughing, but laughing at other things. She won't be able to laugh at boys or men but she'll laugh at loneliness, she'll laugh at her wrinkles in the equally wrinkled mirror and one day, carrying a bag of groceries in each hand, on the way back to her meager quarters, she will stumble in the street and fall, cursing her plentitude, laughing when death allows her consciousness the distance.

11
SUMMER WITH MICHAUD

For the first time in a while not enough family is living with us. Which leaves the front bedroom free to let. Mother loses no time in renting it and chance has it that it goes to Michaud. Just Michaud. I can't recall the first name and that is characteristic, not so much of me, though it might be, as of Michaud. (Recently, when I had occasion to spend some time with Rodolfo, I happened to remember to ask and he, who always had an excellent memory, could not recall.)

Michaud is as nondescript a forty-year-old Canadian male as one ever wants to meet. For a time, after Michaud, I even carried the prejudice that descript Canadian males might not exist. Not that he is a failure, for failures are marked as such for having attempted something. Not a failure but, of course, not a success either. Just a man comfortable enough with some saved money to be out of work during a summer when temperatures in wartime L.A. have soared into the 90's and show no signs of backing off. The voices on the radio sound as if literally coming out of the heart of warm varnish and wood. Not a breeze stirs the curtains and we humans would like to find a way to get out of our suddenly overly thick skins.

Michaud moves in with a suitcase in each arm and an old Stetson very high atop his curly reddish hair. Smiling. He comes in out of the sun soup sweaty but smiling sideways at me and making a beeline for his room, which is off the living room and which Mother had already shown him that morning. He smiles and is gone. Soon he reappears with only a towel wrapped around his midriff, goes into the bathroom for a shower and exhausts all our hot water. But Mother shrugs. Who needs hot water in August?

In the late afternoon a Michaud in a short sleeve Hawaiian print shirt and Bermuda shorts and sandals emerges from his room. I am sitting in the living room and we begin to talk. He sees the book on my lap and we talk about Romain Rolland for a while.

"French writer, right? Pacifist?"

"Yes, right."

"Ever read Emil Ludwig?"

"No, but I know he's good."

"I have one of his books. A bio of Balzac. Very good."

"I'd like to read it…"

"I'll sell it to you, for a dollar."

"I don't want to buy a book." I say, put a little off guard by the outright offer.

"You can borrow it then," he says unruffled. And he goes and gets it for me.

In a month I know that Michaud doesn't stand a chance of ever being like other human beings. He's too detached, too easy going, too optimistic and starry-eyed to be human. He'd be Whitman if to be that *camerado* you didn't have to lift a finger. As it is, he is Michaud and we haven't gone anywhere with him and never will. It is not as if he's thawing after forty years in the Arctic wastes; he has vegetated in California for some ten years now. But this doing-nothing without this nothing becoming disgusting or vulgar in any way must go back to childhood because it is too ingrained, it permeates his entire personality. He is a do-nothing man, looking to do nothing seriously. Hunger is the only motivation, the only breeze that stirs the leaves of this tree. And hunger has been placated for a while.

In the garden the snails have sealed themselves off on the swollen limbs of succulents. Under Michaud's windows, masses of ferns subsist in their wiry, stubborn way as if under the influence of opium. The entire town dozes away or has slipped off to the beaches. The streets are deserted except for a few unsavory characters and roustabouts. One sees incipient bag ladies (the term will not come into use until forty years later!) crossing streets for the sake of a shade tree on their way to hopeless errands. If one passes in front of a bar on the Boulevard, a bar with bamboo curtains for a door, the exhalation of stale and spilled beer mixed with concentrated cigarette smoke, is like the repugnant breath of a decadent dragon. In the dusty, second-hand bookstores, Nietzsche and Schopenhauer want to expand at the expense of Ling Yutang and lesser personalities. The air inversion is so extreme that the smoke from the backyard incinerators turns into a tear-producing eye irritant whether you stay indoors or not.

Under these conditions, Michaud's lifestyle makes sense. Do as little as possible, move no more than alligators do at the zoo, and drink Kool-aid. Kool-aid is for Michaud everything that wine and beer and coffee and tea and plain water are for everyone else. At a nickel a package he must spend I'd say thirty to forty cents a day just to keep himself in liquids. What he eats, on the other hand, is a mystery. He has no cooking privileges in our house but is allowed to keep some cold meats in the fridge. I guess he stuffs himself with bologna. I do not investigate into this matter any further because I detest cold meats, especially the ones with assorted sections of semi-transparent reds and ochres. You just know that several species of animals each provided several different parts and organs to create those squarish extravaganzas one is supposed to ingest. For Michaud, however, there are no categories where food is concerned. Everything that is food is food, to be eaten with divine indifference. It is his soul that transforms quantity into quality. He caught Mother throwing away some stale bread one day and suggested that she turn over all such rejections his way. Green mold is good for you, he insists.

I think he is secretly waiting to be discovered by the movies. He takes walks along the Boulevard in a conspicuous way. It is hard to say how walking can be made conspicuous without becoming weird or borderline but please take my word for it. Michaud can do it. The head, the eyes, the carriage... Something both transcendent and immanent is obviously begging to be discovered. He looks enough like Danny Kaye to conceivably be his stand-in in some scene involving danger and so he imagines that Danny's agents are daily combing the Boulevard for just such a man. I base this on one remark he let drop one day. He said to me, "You know, I could be Danny Kaye..." He had just stepped away from a full length mirror in a window of one of the Boulevard stores. I laughed but he didn't, he made a gesture with one hand as if to say, "...well, think about it!"

I have gone with him on a few occasions and it's like walking with a male goose, everything head gestures and looks in all directions. Done with a certain flair and not enough to put him into the category of the definitely eccentric. But most peculiar: he makes or is friends with every motorcycle cop on the way. These beefy gentlemen are parked on most street corners and are distinctly unapproachable but Michaud makes a beeline for them. He stops to chat with them while their black uniforms give off the feeling that all of Oklahoma is roasting nicely inside each outfit. Michaud expounds on his 5-5-5 plan to everyone, but especially to these cops who, he thinks for some reason, may be the deciding factor when the inevitable breakdown of the society takes place.

The 5-5-5 plan is entirely Michaud's own invention and he proposes it as the panacea for all the world's ills. Stunning in its simplicity, the plan means that every able-bodied man and woman works five hours a day for five dollars five days a week. Period. Under no conditions will any exceptions be made. Sometimes, thinking about his chimera, Michaud gets excited enough to project writing letters to Roosevelt, Churchill, Stalin, and Chiang Kai Shek but the difficulty of finding their addresses makes him postpone the dawn of true human civilization.

This plan is at the root of Michaud's hearty self image. Having thought of it makes him feel justified in his existence. That's why he can walk around town grinning like a benefactor and brimming with *bonhomie*. One doesn't give him a doughnut for fear that his happiness will prove too much and that something might snap in that supple brain tap-dancing on the thin flooring of world renovation.

I mention doughnuts because I connect them somehow with a childhood memory of reciting Simple Simon for my grandmother's benefit and with seeing an illustration for Hot Cross Buns on the opposite page to the rhyme I had so cleverly memorized. With Hot Cross Buns I had imagined an English landscape with Simple Simon cavorting and stealing buns and doughnuts. Michaud partakes of the extended dreamlike, fairytale-like, qualities of Simple Simon and harlequins in general. At least in my mind. Attractive idiocy comes to mind. The Fool of the Tarot cards. Walking about destitute in an 18th century England of fat merchants and red-liveried servants. Michaud there for all his French blood.

I am exploring mysteries. A man who is a distinct nobody read across ganglions of memory in order to set faint harmonies in motion. In this field of thin character sleuthing any little thing serves. Like finding the words *adjutant* and *scaffolding* written in pencil on a slip of paper in the middle of the Balzac biography. They have no bearing on each other so they can only have been at one time new words in his vocabulary or words he had trouble spelling and wanted to pin down.

The words take on the enigmatic nature of characters scrawled ominously on a brick wall. I know they are not going to reveal anything at all. For one thing, I am not Sigmund Freud. Secondly, more infuriatingly neutral words could not be imagined. And yet… And yet… I may be only looking for the three feet of the cat, as we say in Spanish, but isn't there a whiff of subservience to the words, especially to adjutant? A preference for military hierarchies perhaps? Or is that too obvious? But when followed by scaffolding one gets to thinking. Chance here would be buttressing psychological dependencies, the obscure side of this apparently angelic non-entity, this harlequin inhabiting the shiveringly pink forest of a Rousseau painting.

I don't know. I like Michaud but I don't like the words adjutant and scaffolding. Scaffolding I might have liked once but now I only use it out of sheer necessity. As in near constructions, when it's prudent to check any scaffoldings first before walking under them. In doing so one has to, naturally, think the word scaffolding. In the poems I have begun to write I like to torment words by changing their vowels or adding consonants, as in Siptamber for September and finfant for infant. Scaffolding would have been a good word to change in this way, perhaps in a poem about a hanging. Michaud certainly comes through as a man who might incite fate into perpetrating a hanging. Had he lived a hundred years ago he might have been one of those horse thieves they strung out on the branch of a tree, the only scaffolding the oh so unsolid air between the hanged man's feet and the ground.

But more perfect still is the vision of a harlequin hanged by an adjutant. The harlequin has been flirting with the adjutant's woman on the outskirts of the camp and the adjutant has managed to bring charges. It is a time of war and hanging Frenchmen is almost a sport. Michaud pushes Danny Kaye aside and plays the role perfectly. The saintly (and saintily enamoured) harlequin forgiving his tormentors as they lead him up the scaffolding while the adjutant's woman is home weeping over this unfulfilled love that offered her buttercups when she was used to fisticuffs.

One day Michaud leaves. He cannot afford our rent any longer and, anyway, my cousins Mireya and Cecilia are coming to the States and will require the room. Michaud leaves with his two suitcases and the sidelong smile at me, a perfect repeat of the first one. He leaves the Emil Ludwig book with me, must travel light.

The following summer he's back again. Just to visit, to touch base. He is a little thinner, hasn't had a chance to shave. Mother offers him five dollars if he'll crawl under the house to retrieve our cat. The cat is dead a few days and has been stinking up the house. Dead because I inadvertently sprayed him with insect repellant too heavily thinking to rid him of his fleas.

Michaud estimates that the job is going to make him sick to his stomach for a day so, besides the five dollars, he wants a meal before he meanders into the crawl space under the house. Mother cooks him eggs and bacon and serves him several cups of coffee. He talks about his travels but there is a wisp of lying in the air. He makes it all up, he's been nowhere. Finally, his tales over, his travels done, he prepares. He dons one of Mother's old dresses, puts rubber gloves on and, with the air of a man sailing for darkest Africa, unscrews the small screen window under the kitchen and goes in. He carries a flashlight and a large paper bag; nothing is missing. The expedition should be a success. But the minutes pass, our calls go unanswered. Finally I crawl after him, without the benefit of an additional covering, without gloves, without a flashlight. Our blessed little man has fallen asleep ten feet from the cat!

I leave him there to sleep, take the paper bag and finish the job. Painful as it is to find our once beautiful cat swollen like a rubber ball, the stench calls for action. I get him into the bag and get out fast. Into the garbage he goes. Then we wait. Michaud emerges around six in the evening, puzzled, a bit shame-faced, with empty hands. No, we assure him, the cat's got to be there. Didn't he himself comment on the smell? He says he has searched all over and can't find the animal. He is in a panic that he won't get the five dollars. We are having dinner so we invite him to sit down. He can't understand why we are in such high spirits, he has never seen Mother and Father laughing so much. He wants to tell us that laughter is better at another time, that feeding is serious business, but I wink at him and he just smiles and reaches for a second helping.

12

THIRTEEN TANGOS FOR STRAVINSKY

RUDOLFO MOVES TO BATON ROUGE TO STUDY at the university there. He is replaced, at various times, by two of his brothers (one, Mario, with wife and child), and by sundry cousins from my mother's side of the family. The house is more than full, with sometimes my sister or me having to sleep on the living room couch, depending on the gender of the guests, but it never seems crowded or unbearable. The bathroom is always available and one can find solitude in either the living room, the kitchen or the backyard garden. It has to do with having come from a matriarchal setup. In Costa Rica, most of our family, consisting of three fully represented generations, managed to live under one roof perennially pounded by rain and hard times with great equanimity. In an environment run by a grand-mother and grand aunts, one learns the beautiful art of being self effacing if not partially invisible. This brings grace with it, a trimmed ego and a conviviality that the atomized Ameri-can family has not known since the middle of the last century.

Still wondering how to get a grip on music, I began reading a book on acoustics, of all things. I try to like it but the science of sound has nothing to do with what music has been doing to me ever since I started listening to it. When the going gets rough I fall back on the lassitude of Whitman. I take him with me up into the Hollywood hills where I hunt for identity. His words propose exactly what the smells of earth and resin, the insect buzz and the calls of birds suggest I do with my life:

Drown it in essences. Directly. But then, that's easy for Whitman. Easy for insects and birds.

On the other hand, because Romain Rolland's novel *Jean Christophe* is so bulky, I can't take it to the hills with me. I read it in the cool of the late afternoons, sitting on the front porch of our house.

Science is out, though my parents hardly suspect it. I want to write music but I don't have the nerve to announce it outright. Father and Mother still believe that I am going to study bacteriology even when I convince them to let me swap my microscope for an upright piano that I see advertised in the paper.

When the upright comes, wheeled in by two burly men, we discover that it really is an elephant is disguise, one with a bronchial condition. A beast one must be kind to. Whereas what I do, since I know nothing, is bang away at it, wallowing in dissonances that Mrs. Jorganson next door bears with Teutonic dignity. Mother, who once in a while tries to play a waltz she learned as a child, her fingers like a drunk on an icy sidewalk, will hear no complaints. She will always back my explorations, as if having the chance to try anything was the reason why we left the provincial life of a tiny country to come to California.

Bless the fiber of her spirit. Some forty years later, when she's in her late eighties, I will play contemporary music for her and she will listen carefully, then proceed to ask the most intelligent questions, for she has come to this earth to inquire, to thrust not only children but herself forward.

I don't recall who it was suggested Romain Rolland to me. In some ways a drawback, as I come to discover later. What he has done is fill my head with the heroics of art, with the kind of elevated romanticism hard to resist at a young age. So it's just as it was with science. Romain Rolland, just as the biographers of Fabre and Pasteur, has me in a fever to go out and serve humanity with proud weapons.

Now it is even more immediate and overwhelming. I want to start singing right away, like one of those crickets in the hills that plies his fiddle night and day. I want to create beauty, Beauty with a capital B. To be noble and unique like deaf Beethoven. To struggle against philistines, to conquer new provinces... Could there be anything more fantastic? I don't stop worshiping Fabre and Pasteur, merely embrace fresh heroes who, when I listen to them (so directly) make my limbs shake with a kind of fever I had not known before.

To understand this new breed of man I listen every night from eight to ten to the Gas Company's classical music program. It's perfect; they deliver the meat and potatoes. They don't take chances, but since I don't know what those chances consist of, I get my dose of Brahms, the not too late Beethoven, the heart-rending Tchaikovsky, the shadowy heart of Rachmaninov. On Saturdays they switch to opera, dishing up the monstrosities of Wagner and Italian pastry. It's a rich and endless meal, with *Scheherezade* from an East of almond eyes and, from closer to home, the produce of Spain. I listen but I don't know what's happening, how it is affecting me. It comes helter skelter, with no order, no explanations, no sense of history.

At the library, that sweet building near Hollywood Boulevard with its pond of water lilies, I check out a book on pre-Renaissance music thinking that because it talks about the earliest music it will teach me what I need to know. I am sure that if

I begin at the beginning things will fall into place. In this book the music is written in square notes so my first attempts at composition resemble Medieval manuscripts. But the thrust comes from Rolland, that delicate Frenchman Gandhi went out of his way to visit when he was in Europe, for he has equated the writing of music to answering the cloud of gnats that buzz around my head.

The music keeps on coming and I begin to make choices. After Rimsky with his Russian blue sailor's eyes comes the exquisite Debussy; after the indigestible Wagner the unrejectable Jewishness of Mahler. And working backwards from Bach, a whole forest of giants: Palestrina, Monteverdi, Corelli (named Arcangelo because one hears angels in his music).

And before that? Darkness. Peasants with tambourines and sackbuts. Who knows? It's all a madness worthy of gods who for their own reasons chose this earth to have a singing, — earth so full of other things, horned beetles, pasteurized milk, burglarized Indians, cousins newly transplanted to jobs in drive-ins, at Max Factor's—but which sings nonetheless.

Berta Flores' beautiful daughter comes to live with us for some reason. Berta has this magnificent house in the hills but maybe her daughter needs a little more freedom, who knows? Where Mother puts her is a mystery, the house is that full. Really, the house is like a seraglio, filled with not just my female cousins but the most gorgeous Costa Rican girls imaginable.

Berta's daughter tops the bill. This beautiful girl, thin and dangerous-looking as a leopard, is courted by a middle-aged Swedish gentleman who, when he visits, inevitably gives me one of his stupendous cigars. They make me a little sick, but he assures me that the road to manhood goes uphill with many a curve. I smoke a pipe ever since Mother allowed me to, less than six months ago, and only because pipe tobacco is cheap compared to cigars. If I could, I would begin each morning with the smoke from a Cuban cigar, and make the afternoon interminable with another one, and then I'd have a third, reduced to ashes with the day.

I must say there is something unfortunate about this gentleman. He dresses well, wears an aftershave redolent of ease, and yet he is bothered by a little guy like me. He is bothered by the small red flag I have hung over my bed, he is critical of my two paintings which I have painted on discarded window shades: one is of a humanity saved by socialism, the other of a burning garret with a piano and a portrait of Beethoven on the wall. "Liebe und Noth," it reads over his head. "Love and Poverty."

"I don't mind the Russian flag," he tells me. "But why not have the American flag as well? After all, you are a guest in this country."

I don't believe he doesn't mind the Russian flag but what I tell him is that I am not a guest in this country. "This is the earth, Sir. I was born on this earth. I have every right to be here...."

He laughs with a wonderfully healthy laugh, the laugh of one who knows he is all wise, benevolent and understanding. "Then you should have the flag of every single country up over your bed!" he says, wanting to pat me on the head.

"The Russian flag is not just a flag," I argue. "To me it represents a hope that the future is not going to be more of what we've always had...."

"And what is that?"

"Poverty such as one can't imagine for millions, and too much wealth for just a few!" I feel my face burning as I say this. Did Beethoven advocate a different kind of poverty?

He paces up and down the living room. Irma is taking too long in getting ready but I can't just leave him to wait alone.

After a pause, sure enough, he says the inevitable, the thing I cannot bear to hear.

"My dear boy, you are too young. Someday you will realize that human nature is a given; it cannot be changed."

Cannot be changed? Why? Isn't change the unflappable law of the universe? I see that he would consider me impertinent if I went on so I am silent. For that he gives me a cigar. When Irma appears he takes her in with one appreciative look that is as old as the world, and I understand that he owns the world and that he has taught me a great lesson, one I will never accept.

"Your reasoning is purely conventional," I say to him in absentia. At seventeen one doesn't go for balance; at seventeen one wants to make a statement. I quote him brilliant statistics that show the United States is a tight-fisted imperialist power and he backs off, wondering why a pipsqueak like me has a taste for fine cigars. He forgives me my trespasses because his courtship is going well. When it falters we see less of him and I go back to smoking my pipe.

Meantime my cousins multiply even as the bedrooms remain the same number. A gorgeous Carazo girl, from our old Barrio de Amón neighborhood, and two Cleves sisters (from a family Mother knew from childhood on), join them in the struggle to learn English, go to school and work either full or part-time. Cousin Mireya comes home each day amazed at herself for enduring the American eight hour shift at Max Factor's, an unimaginable hunk of feverish time when you come from a Costa Rica where work for middle class girls consists of spending a little time in some bureaucratic office gossiping and waiting for the three-hour lunch, after which more gossip is recollected in tranquility. But she likes it, she makes dollars now.

At a later time, when I will no longer be so keen on changing the world, I will appreciate the fact that Romain Rolland was a pacifist, one of the few French intellectuals to actively oppose WWI. For the time being, I am content or careless enough to imbibe different strains of idealism. After all, the other day up in the hills Walt Whitman said he was proud to contradict himself. Yes, and while I cannot but admire my Swedish benefactor, I have to wonder how far inwardly beyond his impeccable exterior he has ventured. His solidity and urbanity are perhaps only the achievements of a shallow centering. I don't know. I am to find out by going in the opposite directions, by being obdurate, ungrateful and extreme. I need to reject all softness. Down with Chopin, with nineteenth century thunderings. Jean Christophe's larger-than-life existence, swallowed whole, has placed me in a quandary given my ignorance, my limitations and hungers. I smell dangers. Art, which sounded like salvation, is full of pitfalls.

Rodolfo's brother Fernando comes. Again the silk of these Cardona Coopers (Cooper being the mother's side of the family). Fernando is marked by an indelible sweetness, for he is less ambitious and experimental, and more susceptible to daily masks and customs, more vulnerable. Right away he falls in love with the Tartaglia girl around the block, a pretty young thing whose specialty is playing the Grieg piano concerto and whose father, a choleric tailor, insists on playing his 78's collection of classical music more loudly than the composers intended it to sound. His wife, everything he is not, quietly goes about a life of great beauty. She gives me Thomas Mann's *The Magic Mountain* to read and her brother, a shipbuilder from San Francisco, gives me Sullivan's *Beethoven's Spiritual Development* (which, for the sake of the absurd, I go read in a park where the adoring fans of the late Rudolph Valentino have erected a statue to their idol).

With my cousins I begin going to concerts at the Hollywood Bowl. It is summertime and we walk there, talking eagerly, buttoned down by starlight. By the time we reach Highland Avenue and join the droves of music lovers walking to the concert, my excitement has pushed me all the way up in front of my body. Everything takes place within inches of me, itself toppling forward to serve me. The shop windows of Hollywood Boulevard are mine, the bushes that wall up gardens but dispense the odor of roses and jasmine, the traffic, the policemen directing its flash floods, the snatches of conversation, all of it as if it were an initial overture that has transformed the night, an offering turning up all sorts of expectations and shadows. When we get there, the Bowl seethes with electricity, both human and phosphorescently inhuman. Gently rounded tier upon tier of seats begin to fill with people carrying cushions, blankets and thermos bottles. Every person has come to relegate the visual to a secondary role and to use his or her remarkably fixed and immovable ears to taste and wonder at the meaning of the skittish architecture that a hundred men and women construct out of difficult wind tunnels, metal and catgut.

For me, almost better than some of the music, are those few minutes when the orchestra begins to come to life, anarchically, lazily, with some of the musicians trying out little iridescent rills of sound while others hammer away at a single note which, to their lynx ears, insists on being a fraction off, the totality of this a shimmering, chaotic rainbow, a shower of benedictions ignored by everybody but which Charles Ives evokes so well in his Housatonic music (music which I discover so much later).

Now the music's airy softness begins, as if, for the first time, we had learned to make an animal call worthy of our pronounced distinctions. It is a language of our baying at the moon, which has risen as if bidden and has flooded the hills with that pearliness poets supposedly die for; it is a landscape of moisture unknown to the dry yuccas that stand like sentinels in the hills; and it is a dream that we understand like a dream, no more and no less. For it to happen, it has become quiet in the great amphitheater, a thousand breaths hold their breath. Before the conductor raises his baton, one can hear the sizzling of crickets in the chaparral, as if they were clumps of clay and slivers of quartz sighing with relief after the baking heat of the day.

One such night Stravinsky mounts the podium and gestures his way through his magically acrimonious music. A Russia of mnemonic proportions attends us with its onion domes buffeted by snow and misfortune, its summery butterflies dictating wings into the unheeding ear of history. It is the Russia of numberless birches standing over a blunder of bones. Stravinsky is as fresh and true as the hidden perennial brook beneath winter ice. But one can only wonder how such elegant dances, dances of wit and wisdom, can come from this little man as surprising as a wizened Mozart. He flays, entreating this and that group of instruments, begging the bassoon to forget its hiccups, the clarinet to hover over a string tremolo like a reluctant hummingbird, the piccolo to perch on the highest branch of the questioning tree...

At intermission the miraculous happens. Fernando has a press card from Costa Rica and, with it, we are allowed backstage, a dark open area of the Bowl. There, not ten feet away, stands a small Stravinsky of flesh and blood talking to a few people as if he were merely human. Impossible not to accost him. With gallantry he agrees to give me his autograph and I hand him the book I've been studying on acoustics to sign. He is startled and looks at the book suspiciously.

"But I cannot sign in this," he says, looking at me and then all around with his owl's eyes, and speaking with a heavy accent. "It would seem as if I was endorsing someone...."

I take the book back feeling I have committed the worst *faux pas* of my life but he saves the situation. Looking around with quick, birdlike gestures, he spots a tattered piece of paper on the ground and goes to get it. It is a torn bit of newspaper but he signs it, *Igor Stravinsky*, and hands it to me. I sputter with thanks and Fernando and I retreat, the rest of the evening a decided anti-climax.

Fernando or someone mentions that Stravinsky has written some strange-sounding tangos and we are all amazed at this. Tangos are what my beautiful aunt Odilie and my not quite as beautiful aunt Graciela were always scrunched over the radio listening to. I even saw my mother cry when the news came that Carlos Gardel had been killed in a plane crash. And I knew why, too. His voice was the epitome of the tango, it ventured into the jungle of sentimentality with the courage of a man who will go to bed with the woman who detests him, just to prove to her that he doesn't care if she kills him in his sleep.

What is Stravinsky doing in Argentina, the land at the opposite ends of the globe? Has he turned into a gaucho? Is he going to rope the stray cattle of the sky with the long smoky rope of a pampas camp fire? I can't get over it. And then I conceive the notion that I'll write a bunch of tangos and that I'll bring them to him. For months I go on accumulating notes, trying to fit melodies into the abrupt rhythms of our African heritage. The daydream is, naturally, that I write magnificent stuff, that I go visit him at his Beverly Hills house and that he takes me to the piano, where he goes over my music, astonished and enthusiastic. I go home, copy thirteen of them meticulously, and dedicate them to him.

Or to *Petroushka* of the moonlight. To the harlequin of Rousseau. To the clown of *City Lights*.

Tangos which I never write. Which I can't from wanting to so much.

13
LOVE AGAIN

Once again, without warning, I fall in love. Hopelessly, unattainably. With a girl of large, liquid eyes whose gaze is never fixed outwardly because the riches are greater within.

Why now? Why like this? On buses and street corners as if it had to be rationed and one had to live on the limited joys of the exiled? For some reason having to do with the way I am, shy and unworthy, it has no other way and it comes I don't know exactly when with her face, yes, with sight of her, with the repetition of days, the laceration of desire, the nearness of her being with its distances, its horizons. So that I never speak to her.

She gets on the Wilshire and Crenshaw bus and gets off with me at Olympic, where we transfer to the bus that takes us to L.A. High; not every day, only on the good days, the precious days when our paths have been intertwined by levers and heavenly pulleys manipulated by bored archangels with nothing at stake.

I never speak to her, having no occasion to do so, and no nerve; for a long time I'll always assume that girls will be offended if I show the least interest in them. My libido is drowned in guilt. Perhaps merely in shame. I am just not worthy. With this girl I can only stare at the astonishing freshness of her face by remaining in the background or to one side of her. I look at the endless perfection of her features from as many angles as one can obtain by sitting in the back of the bus.

She has dark hair and a pale complexion, wears sweaters, the skirts of a teenager and two-tone shoes. She carries her school books pressed against her chest and, being who she is, this makes her more appealing. She may be shy but I have no way of telling. She must know I do nothing but gaze at her when I can get away with it because from time to time (I have to assume this) it's not her dream that tints the world but this world, my world, that affects her. Then she smiles ever so slightly, so faintly that one has to become expert in this shifting of dreams to be able to detect it. She smiles this way as if telling me it's all right that I adore her. Such an unconscious smile cannot stand survival if our eyes meet so we both try to avoid this. I because I will blush for five minutes and she because I am a stranger, a Latin kid perhaps a hair shorter than she is and perhaps ill with some rare kind of permanent tropical fever.

And so it goes. For months. In the afternoons I ride home alone; she must take more classes than I do, or less. Or perhaps someone in the family picks her up. I have tried varying the time I catch that afternoon bus all the way to one hour later, to no avail. So I am reconciled to the morning's gift, when it is a bit chilly and she is surrounded by a halo of suspended frost suggested by the angora hair of her sweater.

As I say, we get off the Vine bus and cross over to wait for the Olympic bus. We stand at the street corner then, demurely protected from ourselves (from me!) by a small number of black women on their way to their housework in affluent homes. We, all of us, stand there like differently colored Giacomettis while I practice the difficult art of telepathy, pushing hard to have the message leap over the silence. And, surely, something gets across. The smile by which I know her is a state of the art receiving set, even when it would barely register on the horizon of the average assumption as anyone's definition of a smile.

Telepathically, I send my voice, my admiration, to land on her shoulders. The cashmere sweater she is wearing only adds a foreign softness to them, a blurring in which one gets caught as in desired webs. It is in the nature of the imagination to caress this material at will. And to speak, as a bird sings next to the ear of the north, saying, "Your shoulders complete your body's thrust upwards because, in curving to form your neck, they say something so fine that from there on there is no flesh but rather something of an inspiration rejoicing in form." I sing your shoulders because they so kindly allow my gaze (which is everything ever) to rest upon them as if with trinity feet, with whispers of proximity. Once, you moved the right side of your hair aside with the back of your hand and I saw your ear, like a shell tossed by the sea upon a beach without footprints.

The best moment comes when the all-too-soon-to-arrive bus screeches to a halt for us and I have the exquisite sensation that I am about to touch her, that I could and might and shall. We let the black women get on first then I defer to her. She passes within inches of my body, climbs the two steps of the bus and hands the driver her transfer while all this time I am within her gravitational pull, passing through a space that was legitimately hers last and is now bequeathed to me as a clear gift.

Even better yet: once in a while the bus is filled to capacity and we have to stand next to each other, holding onto the overhead bar, balancing ourselves and our books, actually bumping shoulders some of the time, and pretending, pretending to be oblivious to each other. How sad then to arrive at our destination, to let her go, lost among a wash of fellow students as inane and self-contained as fish in a fish tank.

Then time puts on its dentures and goes to work on the heart like a rodent. The classes turn into infernal processes where nothing is done and suffering is an exercise in slow motion.

And the months nibble then devour each other. January feeds on November and a December riddled with holidays. February the swift then makes mincemeat out of January. I keep a coded record of the days I see her. On an otherwise innocuous calendar I mark those with a star and add an extra one if she has glanced at me or if we have accidentally brushed against each other.

On the weekends I escape to Griffith Park, wander the hills and, surrounded by the heat of the chaparral, lie down in the weeds and read a few lines from *Leaves of Grass*. Whitman's poems are all I've got. All else is in abeyance: the music I can't write, the yearning that is almost impossible to encompass with my skin.

With spring I already know the end is in sight. Summer will come and school will be out. The thought of one day soon not seeing this nameless girl every morning is unbelievable even if I could manage to fill my life with plans and promotions.

But I must have an angel of survival that checks things over my shoulder. One day at school the most unexpected thing happens. This elusive girl I lose sight of each morning no sooner we step out of the bus is standing in line in the quad at lunch time waiting to purchase her bus discount booklet just as I am, three students behind her. The shock of seeing her reverberates through me and then I realize what an incredible blessing this is: I will finally learn something about her, where she lives, yes, because one has to sign a sheet for the bus passes, one has to list one's name and address.

I think this and then it hits me: the address is fine, absolutely wonderful, but the name, her name! She's going to let me know her name!

With a kind of impatience that is mixed with terror I wait for it to be her turn. What if she remembers something and leaves the line? What if when she gets to sign it's the bottom of the sheet and the employee there replaces the list with a brand new one?

Nothing catastrophic like that happens. In a universe oiled to perfection it is finally her turn to sign, pay and get her booklet. Then she is gone. My excitement is such that I am the one who might have to leave the line, betrayed by my bladder. But I wait, a hundred muscles in my midriff holding the line. Finally, I come to the window and there's the sheet. I count back. Her name is Jo. Such utter simplicity. Jo Woods. And she lives on Van Ness. Perfection. I spend the rest of the day and the two following ones in a sweet daze. As soon as it's Saturday I check a map and jump on my sister's bicycle (I don't own one, never having seen the need for a gadget like that till now). It takes me about thirty minutes to bicycle from Hollywood to the Wilshire area and then I get to pass in front of her house, sacred territory that I approach with awe, pretending indifference in case she's behind the window curtains. It is a corner house, large, of stucco and a heavy wood frame, painted in a light, yellow ochre.

I pedal past, saying the name Jo to myself with each tired thrust of my legs. I have, for all intents and purposes, turned into a Tibetan prayer wheel. I have reinvented the repetition of mantras. Jo is a wonderful mantra, short, positive, to the point. The J sound is particularly attractive, a friction before the relaxation of the giant O that encompasses everything. Jo Woods is even better, sonorous, noble, impenetrably good and medicinal. I say it so many times I have cured all present and future illnesses, all bodily contumely.

I am asked where I have gone on the bicycle all morning, it's that unusual, and I answer that I was exploring the city. I don't tell my parents it's not the city or my city that I explore but her city, her neighborhood, her street, the way the sun surrounds her world with a quiet calm, having to tan her ivory skin through the windows of her room. I'd give anything to know which windows on the second story are hers.

The following Saturday I take off again. Now I am even hoping that I'll catch a glimpse of Jo in her yard, or that she'll see me pass by and assume I live in the neighborhood. Who knows, maybe then she'll have to ask me, on Monday morning, as she boards the bus, if I don't live impossibly near.

But I don't see her and she obviously doesn't see me or doesn't dare ask. This peculiar courtship has been languageless, totally unacknowledged and we are frozen, I in my games of ecstasy, she in her who knows what thoughts of me, if she has them at all.

Oh, but she must have them, even if tiny, even if insignificant. Thoughts like, "Oh, there he is again, without an umbrella." One doesn't share buses, street corners and school for a year and not wonder. Perhaps she is convinced I am a deaf-mute.

To eliminate this worry on her part one day I tear off part of my bus transfer and, when we board the Olympic bus, I behind Jo, I tell the driver I am sorry but I've lost part of the thing. I say it in my huskiest voice even though it cracks in the middle and I have to finish the sentence in my regular voice.

And summer comes, it is just around the corner. When everyone is photographed for the yearbook I realize that her picture will be in it so I rush to buy it. I have her and I don't: I find that she's a year ahead of me, a member of the graduating senior class and the pain of that takes away the pleasure I get from possessing her likeness. I know for sure now that all I have is one week of her left. And what's worse is that for two days of this final week I miss seeing her.

On the last day, the very last, there is a carnage of school hours and then it's all over. I have not seen her and all I have left to do is cross the big front lawn to the bus stop while everyone else is cheerfully calling out good-byes, delighted that school is out at last.

I arrive at the bus stop. Three girls are waiting there, girls I don't even glance at. But something makes me look again, one of the girls turns, and it is Jo. I calm down as best I can and, summoning up all my courage, I take my school annual and ask her to sign it. Yes, I speak to her, I say,

"May I have your autograph?"

No! I almost say that but I am not a complete idiot. I say,

"Will you sign my yearbook?"

And she says,

"Sure!"

She smiles a full smile, greater than all the mysteries of her previous veiled gifts, and lowers the books from her breasts. I place the yearbook on the books and hand her my pen. She scribbles something, all the time maintaining that large, genuine smile.

Now the bus is almost upon us. I am dazzled but have enough presence of mind to retrieve the yearbook even if it is with trembling hands. I can't say anything else to her. What could I say? The only possibility would be to stutter with clumsy words and horrify her. No. Give me the path of silence; words have nothing to do with a moment like this one, such a late, miraculous moment.

She has written, "Best wishes, Jo Woods," the words she had to write, the only thing she could say. I don't hold them against her because what she has really signed, on the blank page of my astonished luck, is a covenant between us that acknowledges this history of respect and silence between us. And I know she knows this because I have asked for her signature and she has seen the effort it took to do so.

It is over, but I have triumphed over my oceanic shyness, over whatever I thought she thought of me. And with this tiny but most excellent and otherwordly triumph I go home to face the slowly fading picture of my idiot love for her, love that was real to the degree that my eyes owned her and when the unevenness of the streets could make a bus sway and bring us into physical contact with each other. As if she belonged to me more that way than by her having taken possession of my mind and heart and sinews.

It's a long way the summer has with grieving when the green world's green and nobody's for sorrow. The wind coming from somewhere far rides the waves of the ocean and soars over Los Angeles, over the puny dried flower of my malady. And surely, one day at a time, over decades, I will continue serving as clerk to chaos, secretary to disaster. Knowing that there's nobody with my particular coordinates I'll be that useless, wayward man to shepherd memory out of its abandoned tenacities. Life will pass in the doing, the wind will go on riding with the waves, galloping with its jubilant hooves over dust, over the wrinkled earth, under constellations timeless with perplexity.

EPILOGUE

In his introduction to *Speak, Memory*, Valdimir Nabokov addresses the difficulties he had in recollecting events, names and dates, and how, finally, after much concentration or after discussing certain events with his cousin or sisters, things became clarified. He seems to have reached the point where he was satisfied that the correct name or place or time had been pinned down like one of his many butterflies.

I, on the contrary, have found myself remembering less the more I think of things and though I too have a cousin and a sister who have clarified some items, the great bulk were outside their time frame or circumstance, and I had to travel alone.

But beyond that, an exact recollection is an impossible thing. Especially so if one has come to see that reality itself is as multi-faceted as the colors that emerge from the diamond's single drink of light. Participants give it different emphases. Time nibbles at the edges. What was once a definite reality fades into a memory that is peculiarly mushy and indistinct.

This memoir represents an honest attempt to reach back and reconstruct a past. And I have wanted to honor that past by utilizing the full measure of the language available to me through fifty years of writing poetry in English. So these remembrances on paper are not reductivist precisely because, to cling to the diamond metaphor, I wanted to retain all the colors; even the color of color. To say it another way, one's life is a fable structured in accordance with one's beliefs and sensibilities. To have lapsed into a realism proper to journalists would have been dishonest, for the truth is a nugget that must be polished until it breathes.

The happenings in this book are orchestrated by the timeless machinery of affection. To find oneself back in a particular year and age partakes of the disorientation one feels in a strange city when one has to ask somebody where the west lies. Rather than the accuracy of a non-existent compass, I have followed a better guideline, namely the heart. It was disorienting to have my cousin Rodolfo tell me recently that he and Michaud had the job of distributing phone books in the Hollywood hills one summer (disorienting for two reasons: one, because I had forgotten that their particular stays with us coincided and, two, because I had forgotten with whom it was that I had been when I saw the persimmon tree mentioned in the second tango. His talk of this brought back the fact that I had been with them for a few days helping with the distribution, house to house, of telephone books in the Laurel Canyon area.

Readers who seek the perfection of fact in memoirs ought to give up at the start. I, for one, have delivered telephone books up and down the hills of Los Angeles, taking a break to steal persimmons from a hillside, but I can't deliver the immensity of the loss that is memory.

I have chosen, instead, to leave Rodolfo and Michaud in their separate places the better to concentrate on what each of them meant to me. If the fable is incomplete or slightly rearranged, the myth is certainly true to fact and affect.

I grew up hiding in a rich and confusing thicket of consciousness, peeking out with the passion of a Peeping Tom. The only thing that interests me is beauty, its various metamorphoses. I have wanted the reader, if he has persisted to the end, to recognize in these pages some of the beauty it takes to survive one's youth, to recall the monstrous loss of that person to that someone now so different and so equally at a loss, older and nearer the big shift to darkness.

About the Author

Alvaro Cardona-Hine was born in 1926 in San Jose, Costa Rica. When he was thirteen years old, his father was appointed honorary consul from Costa Rica and the family was transplanted to Los Angeles.

His thirteen previous titles include a translation of Cesar Vallejo's *Spain, Let This Cup Pass From Me* (Red Hill Press, 1974), *Agapito*, (Charles Scribners' Sons, 1969), and *A History of Light*, (Sherman Asher Publishing, 1998) which was named a Small Press Book Award Finalist for 1998. He has been awarded a National Endowment for the Arts fellowship in 1978, a Bush Foundation Fellowship in 1978, and a Minnesota State Arts Board Individual Artist Grant in 1982.

His work has been praised by Thomas McGrath for his "astonishing ability," hailed by *Library Journal* as "full of delight, warmth and grace," and *The Bloomsbury Review* writes "...reminds me of the elder Pablo Neruda whose artless language disentombs the magic of childhood...dazzles us with affection and delight."

He began his serious study of Zen Buddhism in 1967, which informs all his creative work : writing, musical composition, and painting. He makes his living as a painter, selling his work from a small gallery in the mountain village of Truchas, New Mexico.